The New Zealand Morris Minor Story

The New Zealand Morris Minor Story

Reiner Schoenbrunn

transpress

ISBN 0-908876-11-4

First published in 2002 by

transpress New Zealand
P.O. Box 10-215
Wellington

transpress@paradise.net.nz
www.transpressnz.homestead.com

Design by Geoffrey Churchman
Printed in Hong Kong

This 1961 model was completely stripped out in 1990 and body repairs done. The paintwork is finished in 2-pack Glazurit paint. It was reassembled in 1993 and has travelled 130,000 miles (209,000 km).

Right: A 1955 saloon, a Series II model, photographed at a Masterton vintage car show in the late 1990s.

Above: This vehicle is a 1952 saloon, fully restored and in immaculate condition.

Left: This 1963 Minor used to belong to a woman hairdresser in Lower Hutt and used as her business and private transport. Rust problems forced it off the road and it is now scrapped.

Left: A 1969 Van that used to belong to the author, now owned by the man pictured, a retired panel beater.

Below: A 1954 Series II traveller. They were never assembled in New Zealand but were a popular "No remittance" import. The split-screen traveller model is today seldom seen.

This 1948 model Tourer, registered in 1949, was completely restored over four years in the 1990s by its owner and has won prizes in local shows. The tourer model was not assembled in New Zealand and only one car was imported as fully built up in 1949 (according to Nuffield export statistics).

Contents

Introduction

More than thirty years ago my school class was taken on a school trip to our neighbouring Holland, supposedly to acquaint ourselves with the culture of this nation. Impressions of huge windmills, vast fields of colourful tulips and picturesque canals have survived in my memories to the present. Another impression that lasted, but much clearer, is that of an at first strange, but then attractive looking car which I spotted parked somewhere in Amsterdam's tranquil side-streets. I had no idea what make of car it was, as it sat there on flat tyres neglected, beaten up, and without any of its badges. It was so different from anything else I had seen previously. The front half was made from beautifully rounded steel, that was usually the case then, but the rear end including the back doors, incorporated wooden framework: that was new to me. This concept, I learnt much later, used to be common in pre-war car making, but until then I had only seen it in the construction of old historic German farm houses. A passing pedestrian must have noticed my interest in the car's lines and explained in Dutch, which I don't understand, all sorts of things about the car — and that it was English, that bit I could make out. Despite his elaborate efforts, however, England and its cars were out of my world then and the identity of the car remained a mystery. I let the matter rest.

About fifteen years later, in 1984, I left my native Germany and visited New Zealand for the first time. Early impressions of a rainy and humid Auckland City were blurred from jet lag, but despite my tiredness, I could not help notice that the place was filled with the same interesting looking cars, now mostly saloon models made from beautifully curved steel all-round. They had my immediate and undivided attention. If people still drive them in this country, I thought, it is already very appealing and, without realising it, my love affair with the Morris Minor had begun!

After six months of holidaymaking I decided to take a job and stay for good. With the first money saved I went to a vintage car dealer to take a closer look at this MM Series Minor that already had cost me several sleepless nights since I first spotted it. To be honest I was already set on buying it before I even got there. The car was cheap and warrantable, I believed, but I later discovered to my disappointment that the sills had an apparent lack of steel and the floor was literally hanging on a few pop-rivets where it really mattered for the Warrant of Fitness test. The engine was so worn that it started to develop huge clouds of smoke prompting other motorists to wave fists at me as "we" tried to negotiate one of Wellington's steepest hills on the way home. Despite my strong belief in the reliability of British cars this one was so abused from its hard work for twenty-odd previous owners that "we" didn't make it and a flatmate had to tow us home. My pride and joy got parked-up alongside the flat to take a little rest. All that worried me very little, I had faith in my mechanical skills, but what mattered the most was that I was the proud owner of my first Morris Minor. The desperate spare parts situation I got into prompted me to salvage many others in similar condition from derelict sections; I tendered for them at the City Council's yard, never refused a donation, and always kept an eye on the "M" column of the second hand car advertisements, which were plentiful back then. Every time I located a new sad case I felt like an archaeologist who just found another skeleton of Moa bones wanting to preserve them for future generations at all cost. My collection of whole cars, half cars, useful wrecks and cartons filled with small parts grew out of all proportion suitable for suburban life; it was in fact so bad that I had to rent several garages in the greater Wellington area which cost me a small fortune. This kind of hording sooner or later attracts criticism from the unconverted and almost needless to say, the majority of landlords did not share my urge for preservation in this manner and did not appreciate the oil stains on the concrete floors. As a result of

Left: The author's first road-legal Morris Minor. Although it looks rough here, repainted later it was a good car for years.

their hostile attitude, moving garage became a regular event. Just when I developed serious doubts about my mental wellbeing I met a group of likeminded people who had done exactly the same for years, which gave me reassurance that I was doing the right thing. It was this group of enthusiasts who later founded the Wellington Morris Minor Club Inc. and I joined as one of the first members.

Eventually I left Wellington and moved to the countryside where my hobby was welcomed with open arms by the farm owners. The more the better, they said, encouraging me, so my collection could grow to about ten whole cars and several truckloads of parts. Admittedly in recent times my urge to tackle frustrating rust repairs and greasy engine overhauls has declined sharply, partially due to getting married and the arrival of family. My collection is now reduced to two and a half cars only, but the interest in the preservation of these cars, more so their heritage, especially the New Zealand side, is still alive as ever. During enthusiast gatherings and rallies I tried to find out more about the historical background of British cars in New Zealand. I wanted to know how they came to travel half way around the world and why they once were so popular and why, generally speaking, they are not now. The answers were mostly unsatisfactory which prompted me to dig deeper in search of the truth. My occasional inquisition gradually developed into a systematic investigation filling boxes with photographs and folders with information about Morris cars and historic details about the company that assembled and distributed them for New Zealand, The Dominion Motors Ltd. Even though my main focus was always on the Morris Minor it soon became apparent that the history of this car could not be separated from DML and its pioneer owners and staff, of whom I was fortunate enough to meet some in person.

Now, after four years in preparation, with hundreds of letters written, endless phone calls made and thousands of kilometres travelled, some by Morris Minor, the story had painfully taken sufficient shape in my computer to think about presenting it for publication. Despite all efforts made to record history as thoroughly as possible there may be research errors present or details missing; let's not forget all that happened a long time ago and I had to rely on people's fading memories, but if you the reader know it better, please let me know. At this point I also want to express my gratitude to those people who have freely given many hours of their time to contribute. Without their support, help and cooperation this project would definitely not have got off the ground. It has been fun to do, so I hope you enjoy it.

Reiner Schoenbrunn

Sir Charles John Boyd Norwood: Business Director, Man of Public Affairs and Philanthropist

take up contracting and worked on many big engineering projects. His decision to come to New Zealand on a working holiday, before undertaking work on the great Perth-to-Kalgoorlie water supply project, was to be one of the most momentous of his life. On arrival in Wellington in 1897 jobs were scarce, so Charles Norwood persuaded the Wellington Gas company to allow him to make fancy gas illuminations for the forthcoming celebrations in honour of Queen Victoria's record reign. Though he was not successful in this attempt, it did lead to a job with the company. He worked hard, and some 58 years later became Chairman of Directors of the company which gave him his first job in New Zealand. Always on the lookout for a more suited sphere of activity he acquired an interest in Rowse & Hurrell, a Wellington coach-building firm. He took a lively interest in its affairs and eventually became Chairman of the Board. The business soon flourished; Charles Norwood negotiated the Ford agency for the whole of New Zealand and changed the name of the firm to The Colonial Motor Company. The success of this venture did not stop him from starting his own business under the name of Boyd & Company, an agency for the King and Detroiter, two American makes.

Charles Norwood married Rosina Ann Tattle (later Lady Norwood) in 1904. It was the beginning of a very fulfilled marriage and of a very productive life together. They had four children: Eileen Marion (George) who is best known through her work for the Wellington Free Ambulance, the twins Walter Neville & George Boyd—Walter became his father's successor in the family business, but George died of rheumatic fever when aged 8 years and 4

harles John Boyd Norwood, youngest of a family of six, was born in Gympie, Queensland, Australia, in 1871. Apparently he was a delicate child, but was educated at normal schools. Engineering always fascinated him and even during his apprenticeship he helped to design and build mining safety equipment. This young man, full of enterprise and the spirit of adventure, was attracted by the challenges of the gold fever that was sweeping Australia at that time. He did not find his goals but the experience in the harsh Australian outback prepared him well for the tough years ahead. After his wanderings through Australia he returned to

The Armorial Bearings of
SIR CHARLES JOHN BOYD NORWOOD
of Upland Road in the City of Wellington
and Dominion of New Zealand, Knight.

College of Arms
MCMLIX

G.P.Bellew,
Garter King of Arms.

months—and Edna Caldwell (Swanson), who lives in Australia at the time of writing.

The Dominion Motors history began in 1912 in Wellington, New Zealand, when Charles Norwood founded a company he named The Dominion Motor Vehicles Ltd. From humble beginnings, a rented garage and a small office, he soon progressed to larger premises at Courtenay Place in the capital's business centre. The firm prospered and eventually he put up a three-story structure, the Norwood Building, to become the firm's headquarters. Charles Norwood obtained the agency for Maxwell and Chevrolet brands and soon made the four-cylinder "Chev" a household name in New Zealand. He was responsible for putting thousands of them on the road.

True to himself Charles Norwood tried to hold on to his original policy of handling only New Zealand-wide agencies and eventually relinquished the General Motors line in favour of other brands like Hudson and Essex which

later actually entered into strong competition with GM's top model the Cadillac. American cars were quite profitable and business had been booming until then, but Norwood being of British stock, and proud of it, wanted to put more British cars on the New Zealand market. On one visit to England he sought meetings with leaders of a group of new manufactures but they refused to meet with him. No-one in the United States would have had this attitude, but in the English group he could only meet the assistant sales-managers. The trip was not wasted, because Mr Norwood had the opportunity to meet Sir William Morris (later Lord Nuffield) during a social gathering. Apparently at this point no question of a possible Morris Motors representation for New Zealand was discussed, but surely it was the start of the long personal and business friendship between the men. Some years later the New Zealand based Morris Motors' representative H. Turnley Jones went to see Charles Norwood at his seaside home near Wellington to discuss whether Dominion Motors might take the Morris representation for New Zealand in order to boost vehicle sales which had started to fall during the late 1920s. In December 1930 the agency passed to Dominion Motors and this was the beginning of the firm's long association with Morris Motors Ltd (and later BMC). Sales improved progressively and Morris became the first British brand in New Zealand to head off popular American makes in sales volume.

The Dominion Motors Ltd continued to prosper and Norwood, who had no ambition of accumulating great personal wealth, invested profits back into his Company. What started as a Wellington district project grew into one of the largest and most successful national undertakings wholly owned and financed in New Zealand.

This in itself was an amazing achievement, but being a man with a great appetite for work he looked for other outlets for his energies in intervening years. In 1917 he was elected to the Wellington City Council and served until 1923, but in 1925 he was persuaded to stand for the Mayoralty and was elected. During the two years that he held office Wellington reached a peak of civic progress. Probably one of the greatest services he did for the city was the arrangement he negotiated with the Government to vest in the Wellington City Council some 84,000 acres of land as a water reserve. In recognition of his work he was elected the Suburban Water Supply Board's first chairman.

The 1930s were the years of the Great Depression and nearly everyone suffered economic hardship in various degrees. Those with money were less affected than the poor, obviously, but worst off by far were crippled children. Despite all the Government's efforts they did not receive the care and attention they deserved. Members of the New Zealand Rotary Clubs, of which Charles Norwood was a very committed one, started to realise that and set out to research the possibility of forming a Society similar to the US model first launched in 1913 by the Rotary Club of Syracuse, New York. The District Governor, John Ilott made acquainted himself with the project and within a few weeks under his leadership, committees and individuals were streamlined in their efforts. During a Rotary Conference in Hamilton in early March 1935, the draft constitution and rules for the Society were discussed and the foundations for the New Zealand Crippled Children Society laid. At the same time in Wellington a dinner party was to be hosted by Norwood for Lord Nuffield, who had a world-wide reputation for philanthropy. Norwood left the venue in Hamilton prematurely to meet His Lordship in Wellington at the hotel he was staying for the opportunity of a quiet talk. "I thought," Norwood once put on record, "it an opportune time to ask for Lord Nuffield's assistance and intended to ask for £1000. After submitting a well-considered report, which included a statement to the effect that a survey had been made showing that there were approximately 5000 children in New Zealand not receiving the attention that would bring them to be useful citizens, His Lordship stopped me suddenly and said: 'Do you mean to say that in this beautiful country there are 5000 children who are not receiving the attention that would be helpful to them?' I replied that a survey had been made and that was the information at my disposal. He said, 'Well, Norwood, you will want an endowment for this work. Before I leave this country I shall

Lady Rosina Ann Norwood, circa 1930.

hand you over £50,000 as a nucleus for the service.'"

Norwood suggested to Lord Nuffield that he make this statement at dinner, which he flatly refused to do, but was later persuaded and gave in. "This was the nicest thing that happened at the dinner, which was otherwise a very sociable affair. Lord Nuffield made the statement in quiet, unassuming terms and said just a few words about the unfortunate cripples." The next day the two men left Wellington for Auckland and met the Mayor who brought with him a photograph of the home of Mr and Mrs Wilson who, inspired by what Lord Nuffield had done, offered their home to the cause with no strings attached other than that garden and regular house maintenance had to be carried out. Lord Nuffield thought this was fine and he was impressed by their generosity, however, he could not give a sum to any one particular part of New Zealand but only on a national basis. He promised to leave £10,000 and hoped there would be other gifts of a similar nature. Charles Norwood formed a Special "Trust for Children's Homes" in April 1935, and because there were no other institutions existing

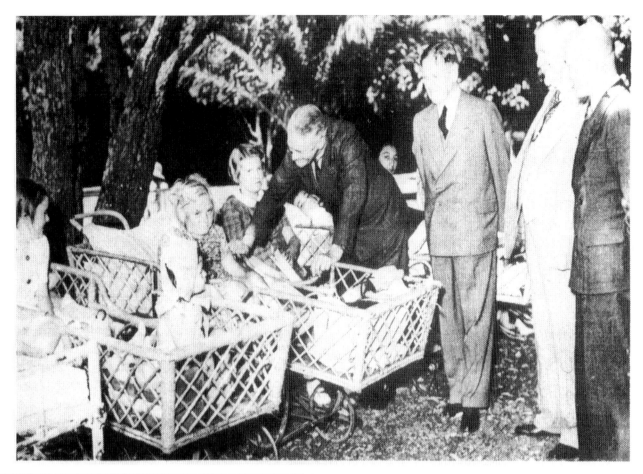

Above: Lord Nuffield (left) visits the Wilson Home in 1945 accompanied by Mr Wilson, Sir Charles Norwood and medical superintendent, Dr C.B. Bilberd.

Left: Lord Nuffield and Sir Charles Norwood at the civic reception given in honour of Lord Nuffield, hosted by the Mayor of Auckland in 1935.

similar to the "Wilson Home," the whole of the money and its interest was paid through the Auckland Crippled Children Society to the Auckland Hospital Board towards the maintenance of the Wilson Home. On his next visit to New Zealand Lord Nuffield was so pleased to see what his gifts had created, that made a further donation of £7500 to the trust. These three donations formed the basis of the Nuffield Trust of which Charles Norwood became the first Chairman. The Nuffield Trust still exists today.

Charles Norwood was knighted in 1937, receiving the accolade from the then Governor-General Viscount Galway as he lay in bed recovering from serious injuries he suffered in a motor accident the previous year. Until then no

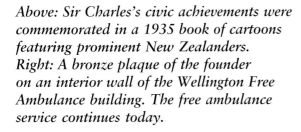

Above: Sir Charles's civic achievements were commemorated in a 1935 book of cartoons featuring prominent New Zealanders.
Right: A bronze plaque of the founder on an interior wall of the Wellington Free Ambulance building. The free ambulance service continues today.

knighthood had been more widely acclaimed in New Zealand. Sir Charles also was a member of the Wellington Harbour Board for 35 years, funded the Wellington Milk Depot, the Fire Board as well as being Founder & President of the Wellington Free Ambulance and the President of the Wellington Chamber Of Commerce, the Wellington Rotary Club, and the Manufacturers Association.

During his long and distinguished career he was also extremely active in welfare and sporting bodies. In 1950, for example, Sir Charles set up a further trust fund, expected to produce £125 a year for children with cerebral palsy in the Wellington area; later the funds were such that they were made available nation-wide. The year prior he made a very generous monetary gift to the Wellington Cricket Association's coaching

fund, again in the nature of a trust fund, which then was expected to return an annual income of around £125. The money was to provide trophies for different phases of the game and, in the words of Sir Charles: "an incentive for cricketers to improve the standard of their play." Emphasis was placed upon the first trophy, the cricketer of the year, the person who combines best with a reasonable ability to play, the true sporting spirit of the game, whether in match play or in practice. The remaining four trophies were to be based upon improvement. The Norwood Trust still operates today and over the years has put around $NZ 1 million into the sport.

Rosina Ann Norwood always took a keen interest in her husband's business and civic affairs. In the ups and downs of the years between the wars, she was his unobtrusive but constant counsellor and evidence of her prudent hand was to be seen in many of the aforementioned activities with which Sir Charles was associated. In 1929 a group of ladies inspired by her got together in the Norwoods' home and formed the so called Wellington Free Ambulance Ladies' Auxiliary of which Lady Norwood became the first President and held office until

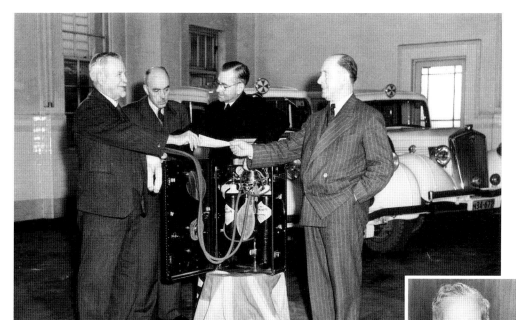

Left: Sir Charles hands over another donation to the free ambulance service in July 1949.

Below: In July 1966, four months before his death, Sir Charles presents a diasonoscope to the Wellington Hospital.

ill health forced her to retire in 1955. Under her guidance and active leadership the organization flourished and raised the funds necessary to equip and run the Free Ambulance Service. Despite a very busy life at her husband's side, archive records show that she rarely missed a board meeting in 26 years in office.

Lady Norwood also had an interest in beautifying the city of her birth, Wellington, in particular the Botanic Gardens. To the Mayor of Wellington she wrote in July 1939:

> Dear Sir,
>
> For several years past I have been one of the many admirers of the Begonia House in the Botanical Garden, and always thought the accommodation was not in keeping with the excellent display the visitors are privileged to enjoy year after year.
>
> I am writing to ask if your Council will accept a contribution from me of £200 to be spent on enlarging and generally improving the glass house.
>
> If acceptable to the Council I feel confident there are many Begonia House admirers who would like to give practical assistance towards making it a really delightful showplace for our City and its Centennial Visitors.
>
> Yours respectfully

The Wellington City Council accepted her contribution and the old glass house was given a refurbish. Many years later in their meeting June 1950, the council decided to honour the Norwoods for their good work and generosity. The following letter was sent by the Town Clerk:

> Dear Madam,
>
> I have the pleasure in advising that the Wellington City Council at its meeting held on the 14th instant decided, with your concurrence, to name the new rose garden to be formed in the Botanic Gardens adjacent to the Southern end of Anderson Park, "THE LADY NORWOOD ROSE GARDEN" in appreciation of the services rendered to the City by Sir Charles Norwood and yourself.
>
> The rose garden when completed will be the finest of its kind in New Zealand and it is hoped that the action of the Council in naming it after you will meet with your approval.

Lady Norwood was delighted, accepted the decision and sincerely thanked the Council for it. Her letter ended with the words: "I will always be keenly interested in this addition to the beauty spots of our City"

Ten years later, on 15 June 1960, the Mayor, Mr Kitts, made yet another announcement during the Council's meeting concerning another, bigger donation from Sir Charles:

> A personal gift of £20,000 has been pledged by Sir Charles Norwood to the City for the construction of a new Begonia House and Winter Garden, … on the condition that work shall begin immediately.

It did. Planning begun hastily and the whole project quickly gained publicity. Already from the end of the month on artist's impressions, drawings of the new complex, and progress reports from the construction site appeared in the daily press. The building was finished and opened to the public on 22 December 1960, Sir Charles himself turning the key and announcing: "…what a pleasure it has been for me, to be allowed to provide this adornment to the Lady Norwood Rose Garden."

The reasons for making such generous gift, and putting a time limit on it, could be several, but most likely Sir Charles felt his own energy dwindling and wanted to create a final long lasting memorial in honour of his beloved wife, who had died in May 1957.

Few during their lifetime have more selflessly served their community, than Sir Charles and Lady Norwood. Age never proved a handicap

to their good work. For example, Sir Charles took his 86th birthday calmly in the middle of a burst of activity spurred on by the Wellington Industrial Fair. Just returned from a holiday visit to his home country, he plunged straight into a round of meetings and functions. In one day Sir Charles conducted an executive meeting of the Free Ambulance Board in his office, then in a hurry checked up on progress at the Industrial Fair, attended and spoke at a luncheon of the Australian Association, of which he was President. In the afternoon he attended the monthly and annual meetings of the Free Ambulance Board and in the evening spoke at the opening of the Industrial Fair. After that he personally conducted the official party around the show, and then escorted them to a function for guests. Asked if he had any birthday comment to make, Sir Charles said: "You're only as young as you feel and I feel pretty good." Whether he had the energy to dance that night wasn't recorded.

Sir Charles John Boyd Norwood died nine years later, on 26 November 1966, aged 95.

An artist's impression of the project, 1960.

The Lady Norwood Rose Garden, part of the Wellington Botanical Gardens. Park benches, fountain, conservatory— nearly everything pictured here has been donated and created by the Norwood family.

CHAPTER TWO

Sir Walter Neville Norwood:
Model Businessman and Philanthropist

Walter N. Norwood (later Sir Walter) was born in Wellington 1907 to his parents Sir Charles John Boyd Norwood and Lady Rosina Ann Norwood. He was educated at Hereworth School (Palmerston North) and Scots College (Wellington). At the age of 28 he married Miss Rana Muriel Redpath (later Lady Norwood) and had two sons named John Boyd and Neville Wayne and a daughter, Jennifer Eve (Brown).

His early experience in business included a training with the Bank of New Zealand and also many visits to leading English and American car factories. Young Walter joined The Dominion Motors Ltd in 1926 as an apprentice in management, working and training next to his father, the Company's founder.

This second-in-command situation remained unchanged even after his promotion to the position of General Manager in 1937 (Director 1940, Managing Director 1958) and it largely continued until his father's death in 1966.

Walter Norwood played a prominent part in developing and expanding The Dominion Motors Ltd to its final size. A milestone in his early career was the order of 3500 Morris vehicles he negotiated 1937 for The Dominion Motors Ltd with Lord Nuffield's export company — Morris Industries Exports Ltd, at a time when numerous difficulties for New Zealand importers were created by quotas and exchange restrictions legislated by Government. Mr Norwood was very much responsible for the establishment of Dominion Motor's two Auckland based car assembly plants (Newmarket 1939 / Panmure 1954), and in 1938 he pioneered the assembly in New Zealand of the first Morris vehicles to be imported completely knocked down.

About 1936 Sir Charles had founded a company he named C.B. Norwood, it was a finance company to provide finance to The Dominion Motors Ltd, with Sir Charles being the Governing Director, and Mr. Walter Norwood the Managing Director. It is understood that Mr. Walter Norwood was in England when in 1947 Mr. Harry Ferguson launched his new Ferguson 35 tractor and Mr. Norwood saw the potential and immediately made a successful bid for the N.Z. distributorship. First shipments of tractors landed just before he himself arrived back in the country. C. B. Norwood Ltd became the trading company selling these tractors and their implements from 1948 on, and it is reported that it did very well for the family over the years, until

A demonstration of the new "Fergie" on a rainy day in 1948, attended by the Prime Minister, Peter Fraser (under umbrella) and C.B. Norwood's General Manager, Ron Webster (right). Walter Norwood (in beige coat) was there too, talking with the PM in the top photo.

in 1978 it was sold to Dalgetys, a Stock & Station company. Some years on a new company was formed which still trades today under the original name of C. B. Norwood Distributors Ltd, but is now wholly owned by Zuellig N.Z. Ltd, with Head Offices in Palmerston North and branches throughout the country. The firm has diversified its activities and long since relinquished the Ferguson (later Massey-Ferguson) brands in favour of a vast range of European farming equipment and the Kubota and New Holland tractors.

After Sir Charles' death in 1966 Mr. Walter Norwood took the Dominion Motors's reins as Chairman of Directors, and it was soon apparent

An historic moment was the meeting of export-ers and importers of Morris vehicles in Welling-ton in 1949. Seated, from left: Lord Nuffield with Sir Charles Norwood. Standing, left to right: Tom Boult, Morris Industries Exports; Walter Norwood, Director of Dominion Motors Ltd; Mr H. Mullen, Director of M.I.E.; Doug Gordon, General Manager, D.M.L; and Arthur Lee, Secretary of D.M.L.

he'd been well-schooled for the task ahead. In the late sixties he foresaw the need for amalgamation of all British-car manufacturers in New Zealand (following the British model, the BMC) in order to form a strong alliance against competition. Mr. Walter Norwood played a leading part in the negotiations establishing the new company, named the New Zealand Motor Corporation Ltd, of which he became first Chairman of Directors. Under his influence the Corporation achieved sales of nearly $89 million in its first fifteen months of operation and Mr Norwood remained in office as Chairman until 1977. During his time the Company first assembled British vehicles under the Morris, Austin, Triumph and Leyland badges, but later shifted more towards the Japanese brand of Honda. By 1976 the New Zealand Motor Corporation had achieved a 27% share of the new vehicles' market in New Zealand and Mr. Norwood continued working as its President until his retirement in 1982. He had recognised as early as 1974 that cosy tariff arrangements for vehicle manufacturing would be threatened by Britain's entry to the EEC. New Zealand's investment in plant and jobs, he argued, would be imperilled. Well, he was right 20 years later the industry he knew has vanished.

Very much like his father, Walter Norwood had interests in other businesses. To name a few, he was a director of NZ Petroleum & Co, a board member of General Finance and Managing Director of the Wool Commission.

Walter Norwood inherited a lucrative business on which he built, but true to his parents' tradition, he was determined that his family would not be the sole beneficiary of the wealth generated. The Norwoods (and later their extended family) sponsored many visible gifts to the city of Wellington, such as the original waterfall, lily pond, the shelter, the wall and

walkways up to the cable car, the tea house, the tropical water lily house and the redevelopment and landscaping of the waterfall/peace flame site in the Botanic Gardens. While this is a great gift to the city of Wellington more, much more was done out of the public's eye in welfare related activities. Huge contributions in terms of financial investment and commitment were made as President of the Wellington Rotary Club, Trustee of the Nuffield Trust, Laura Fergusson Trust and Norwood Crippled Children Trust, to name a few.

During research for this book the author talked to Ernie H. Moston O.B.E. who today still is associated with the Laura Fergusson Trust and cared closely with Walter Norwood for the organization. This is part of what he had to say:

"In 1967 a group of ladies was concerned about the lack of hospital services for disabled people in this country, they decided to start an organization that provided housing and assistance on a 24 hour basis to them, so they could live lives as normal as possible. They persuaded Lady Laura Fergusson to lend her name to the organization. In the beginning it was very much a social thing, also called the champagne and caviar club, primarily for the Ladies of the upper class who had affluent husbands and could pull money out. As part of their fund raising activities the Ladies organized two or three events per year such as Antique Fairs, Black & White Balls and the auction of goods at Government House. If the event was unlikely to fetch at least $10,000, they were not interested, they were big events. The organization flourished and centres were

The New Zealand Motor Corporation board of 1974 with Sir Walter Norwood fourth from the left.

established in Auckland, Wellington and Christchurch. Since its inception the Norwoods have been very regular contributors, donating very acceptable sums of money to the trust, and occasionally when we needed urgently extra funding for a bath-house or spa-pool we asked Sir Walter Norwood personally, he did not mind, he wanted to help — always! He was a humble man who didn't like much publicity in return for his generosity."

Walter and Rana Norwood maintained for some sixty years a very strong affiliation with the Wellington Free Ambulance Service and were extraordinarily generous in supporting both its development and its day to day operations. The Ladies Auxiliary has played a major supporting role to the service. Mrs Rana Norwood joined the auxiliary in 1953 and became a Vice President in 1957–58, 1960–61, 1969–70 and 1975–82. Her hard work and leadership was an inspiration to the committee members. From 1983 on she supported the organization as Patron until the auxiliary was wound up in 1988. The archived records suggest that the Norwoods took the time to attend nearly every board meeting over 35 years!

Walter Norwood also took a keen personal interest in all branches of sport, as a golfer, sailor, motorist and handy cricketer, though in the last case his enthusiasm was not always rewarded with top results. Already in 1949 Sir Charles

established the Norwood Trust that enabled five trophies to be awarded every year to the best cricketers in the Wellington region. Walter Norwood built on the tradition when in 1971 he and the New Zealand Motor Corporation put up the money and trophy for the first inter-provincial one-day 40-over competition. He continued to do so for seven years. Now after more than half a century of existence the Norwood Trust has distributed around 1 million NZ dollars to all sectors of Wellington cricket. The Norwoods made personal annual donations to the Wellington Wanderers Cricket Club and created the "Norwood Room" in the Vance Stand at the Basin Reserve.

Walter Norwood had been a companionable onlooker of his wife's long-time racing interests and got well and truly bitten by the sport. He developed a passionate interest in thoroughbreds, particularly as a owner, and formed a long and profitable association with Awapuni trainer Eric Temperton, one of the best, who was the second person in New Zealand to train 1000 winners. Their relationship reached its apogee in 1971 when Walter Norwood's $7500 investment — Silver Knight — won the Melbourne Cup. Workers were ecstatic and assembly lines in his factories ground to a halt that day. The two men almost repeated the feat the following year when the $6,000 mare Magnifique finished second. In 1972 Silver Knight's racing days were

Sir Walter and Lady Norwood with jockey Bruce Marsh celebrate Silver Knight's 1971 Melbourne Cup win.

over and he was to be shipped to Perth for stud duties, Mr Norwood attended and tried for a stiff upper lip but is reported to have gone "rubbery" when the stallion's box was loaded aboard. His interest in the sport continued for many years

and he became the President of the Wellington Racing Club.

The Norwoods gave so much to Wellington and their name is attached to at least half a century of philanthropy that's worth more than money, much more than millions of dollars!

For his outstanding services to commerce and welfare the Queen honoured Mr Walter Norwood as a Knight Bachelor in 1971, and on 24 March 1995 Sir Walter and Lady Norwood were presented with the Wellington Civic Award by the Mayor, Fran Wilde (pictured). "Wellington City recognises the outstanding and significant commitment of personal time and resource made by Sir Walter and Lady Norwood over many years. Their unstinting generosity to and interest in our community cannot be measured. This Civic Award is a warm appreciation from the people of Wellington."

After 65 years of marriage Lady Norwood passed away in May 1999. Sir Walter died after a long illness in April 2000.

CHAPTER THREE
Dominion Motors Ltd

It was in 1919 that Charles J.B. Norwood, who had commenced a long association with the Motor Industry in 1903 and who had founded his own Company, The Dominion Motor Vehicles Ltd, in 1914, began negotiations with David Redpath of the Universal Motor Company of Christchurch, to merge their two interests into one, The Dominion Motors Ltd.

The firm's capital was increased almost immediately from £120,000 to £140,000 and the newly formed organisation prospered, with Charles Norwood, David Redpath, and E. W. Ackland at the helm.

In 1924 two new branches were opened in Wellington — in Thorndon Quay and Kent Terrace — selling Hubmobile, Clyno, Hudson and Essex vehicles. Two years later the capital was increased to £300,000 and the beginnings of a nation-wide coverage were laid when further outlets were established at Timaru, Wanganui and New Plymouth.

The assembly of cars imported as S.K.D. (semi-knocked-down) began in the Thorndon Quay building in 1927, and the same year further distribution branches were opened at Auckland, Palmerston North and Hamilton. The biggest milestone in the company's history was passed in 1930 when the Morris franchise for the whole of New Zealand was offered to Dominion Motors, which had built-up an excellent sales record. The agreement was reached in December that year and the agency accorded. Thus began an association which not only enabled the Company to establish itself firmly in the volume car market, but which endured to its end.

There were moments of tragedy too. On 14 April 1931, the workshop section of the Kent Terrace premises was gutted by fire. The showroom and first floor areas were not seriously damaged but little was salvaged from what had been Wellington's most modern and best equipped workshop. This was a major blow, but the Company was resilient and recovery was swift.

The depression years in New Zealand were not easy for anybody and the Company had had its share of problems. They necessitated, among other things, the closing — in some cases only temporarily — of a number of branches. Nevertheless the firm's strength and vitality were already such that in 1935 Dominion Motors was awarded a trophy by Morris Industries Export Ltd for being their largest overseas purchaser. In fact it was believed that The Dominion Motors was, at the time, the largest single importer of English cars in the world.

Morris vehicles were popular, sales increased rapidly and the Company was progressing in New Zealand through its connection with Morris Motors Ltd, the latter was also reaping some benefit. This was exemplified in 1937 when Walter N. Norwood, then General Manager of Dominion Motors, engraved the firm's name in the annals of Morris Motors by placing with them the first £1,000,000 order for cars they had ever received. More than 3500 cars were to be shipped to the colony to satisfy the staggering demand. Lord Nuffield personally visited New Zealand in 1937–38 and he regarded the overseas trade possibilities so important that he ordered extensions to the factory at Cowley England, costing more than £40,000. The news was good for both British and New Zealand car workers: it meant 30,000 of them had work for a year or more.

Walter Norwood stated in an interview with an English newspaper: "The motorist in New Zealand wants an economical, low-priced car.

You've filled the bill. We have a fine road system, quite as good as England…but petrol costs 2 shillings a gallon. Therefore the 8 h.p. British car is preferred to the American machine. We sell all cars, but 85% of them are British."

In only five years the exports of Morris vehicles had increased from around 5000 units per year to 30,000 in 1938. But rising shipping costs, and protective duties made it obvious to The Dominion Motors' directors that soon it would no longer figure to import vehicles fully built up. In 1939 the Dominion Motors' first purpose-built plant for the assembly of vehicles from C.K.D. (completely-knocked-down) was erected at

Newmarket, Auckland, and started production. Soon after this, however, the beginning of World War II caused problems with the government imposition of import ontrols, which from then on played an important role in all industries. During the war years Dominion Motors' resources were utilised "for the good of the country" in the manufacture of munitions, assembly of weapons and servicing of army vehicles.

Import restrictions in New Zealand continued for the next 30 years, but, generally speaking, conditions after the war were good enough for the development of a modern motor industry.

The building in Courtenay Place, Wellington, in which Dominion Motors began operation in June 1919. In front are a Detroiter, a Chevrolet and a King.

The Company had its share of good fortune again from 1949 onwards when the Nuffield Universal tractor and the Morris Minor MM, Oxford MO, models were manufactured and distributed through DM's network, which further advanced its already strong market position. Increased production to satisfy the ever-expanding market for cars and commercial vehicles in the early 1950s required a second assembly plant, built at Panmure, Auckland, in 1954.

The industrial equipment side of the Company's activities continued to increase, and in 1960 the department handling that range was separated from the main company and formed into a subsidiary, which from then operated under the name of Dominion Motors Tractor and Industrial Equipment Ltd, referred to as DOMTRAC. Production commenced in a third factory, built also in (then) rural Panmure, designed especially for the assembly of heavy machinery, tractors, earthmoving and road-making equipment. The North Island was serviced by branches at Palmerston North and Wellington, and for the South Island a smaller assembly, sales and service workshop was established in Battersea Street, Christchurch.

Future prospects for the motor industry in New Zealand were looking good at that time and a fourth, large-volume car assembly plant was in the long term planning by 1969 (the land in Henderson, Auckland, had already been acquired), but the building never eventuated through developments leading up to the formation of the New Zealand Motor Corporation the same year.

In 1963 a Dominion Motors branch was established at Lower Hutt, near Wellington, to be followed in 1965 by the resumption of retail operations in Hamilton where the local franchise had been relinquished to a dealer some years earlier. And by 1966 a Tauranga business was purchased and a branch of the Company established there.

Thus in its first 50 years of existence The Dominion Motors Ltd established itself as a major importer and assembler of motor vehicles distributing through seven active branches and a dealer network of 63 nation-wide. Its authorised capital had increased from the original £120,000 to £2,400,000 and its sales moved from the most modest figures in the first year to over £30,000,000 in 1966.

Sadly for everybody involved, the founder, Sir Charles Norwood passed away the same year, but spirit of the man himself, management and staff were looking forward to the challenges and successes of the next 50 years.

A big change was announced in November 1971 when the familiar name The Dominion Motors Limited was replaced by The New Zealand Motor Corporation. Other firms in Wellington who also entered the merger, were Magnus Motors (Austin), the Austin Distributors Federation, in Auckland Seabrook Fowlds Limited (Austin) and several smaller franchise holders around the country. The new company had already been formed in 1969, and shares were offered to the public from then on, but the firms involved had still been trading under their own names until the official announcement. At first NZMC continued the assembly and sales of British makes like Morris, Austin, Leyland, Rover and Triumph, but from 1976 onwards introduced Honda vehicles to their range, which slowly gained market dominance and replaced most of the British brands during the following decade.

Above: The building erected in Thorndon Quay, Wellington, in 1924 served as an assembly depot until 1939.
Right: The retail branch in Timaru.

Lord Nuffield during one of his numerous visits to New Zealand, meeting with Sir Charles Norwood in the mid-1930s.

Right: A full page newspaper advertisement as it was published in Auckland and Wellington in late December 1930. Below: The "Morris Cup" presented by Lord Nuffield in 1935 to DML as the largest customer of Morris Industries Exports Ltd.

The

DOMINION MOTORS
LIMITED
makes an important
announcement

AS from to-day, The Dominion Motors, Ltd. will assume control of the distribution of Morris Cars and Commercial Vehicles in this Dominion. It is well known to the public of New Zealand that Morris Motors Ltd., comprising a group of companies under the control of Sir William Morris, is the largest purely English Company manufacturing passenger cars and commercial vehicles in the World.

The new plan of placing control of Morris Motors' destinies in New Zealand in one set of hands, will make for higher efficiency and lower costs. It has been carried out with the loyal co-operation and help of existing distributors. The complete resources of The Dominion Motors' Organisation, comprising Head Office and ten Branches, together with those of at least 80 Dealers, will be utilised to service Morris Cars and Trucks in New Zealand.

Thus, the largest purely English Company of Motor Manufacturers in the World, will be represented in this Dominion by a Company, the direction, capital and labour of which are supplied entirely by New Zealanders. Profits from the New Zealand sale and distribution of Morris products will remain in this Dominion to swell her prosperity, and the remainder of the purchase price will go to New Zealand's best customer—England!

Call and Inspect full range of Models at our Showrooms, Kent Terrace and Courtenay Place, Wellington ... TO-NIGHT ...

Managing Director,
THE DOMINION MOTORS, LTD.

MORRIS   CARS   AND   COMMERCIAL   VEHICLES

Above: The retail branch in Kent Terrace, Wellington, in the 1930s. Left: A mid 1950s photo of the Dominion Motors head office in the Norwood Building in Courtenay Place, Wellington.

Right: The new assembly plant at Newmarket, Auckland taking shape in 1938-39.
Below: A view taken in the late 1950s.

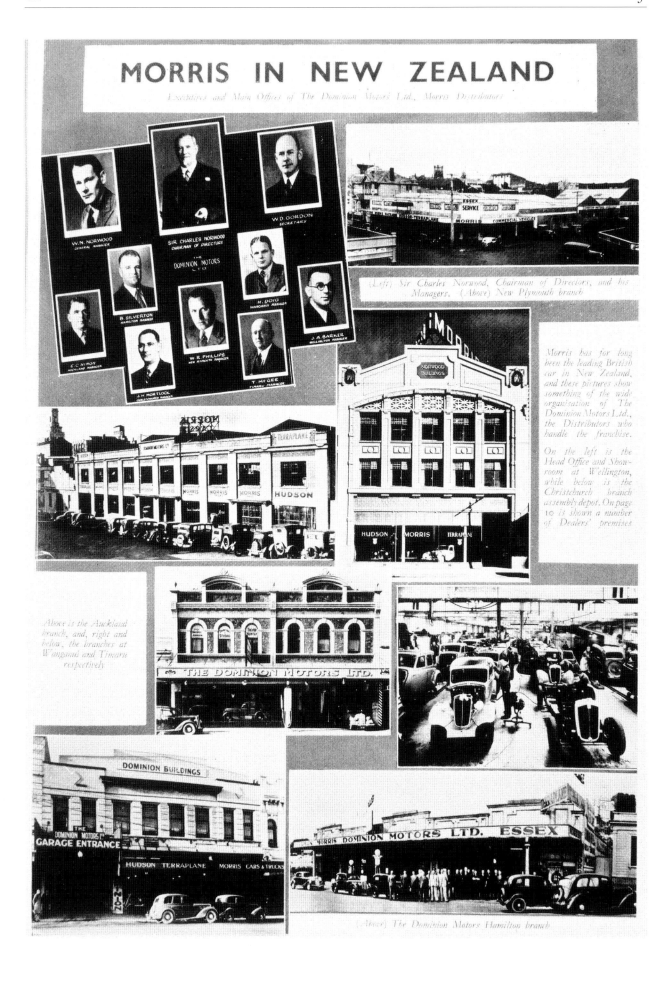

MORRIS IN NEW ZEALAND

Exteriors and Main Offices of The Dominion Motors Ltd., Morris Distributors

(Left) Sir Charles Norwood, Chairman of Directors, and his Managers. (Above) New Plymouth branch

Morris has for long been the leading British car in New Zealand, and these pictures show something of the wide organisation of The Dominion Motors Ltd., the Distributors who handle the franchise.

On the left is the Head Office and Show-room at Wellington, while below is the Christchurch branch assembly depot. On page 10 is shown a number of Dealers' premises

Above is the Auckland branch, and, right and below, the branches at Wanganui and Timaru respectively

(Above) The Dominion Motors Hamilton branch

Many changes took place in the newly formed organisation. A number of people commented during the research for this book that the loveable "fatherly" management style they enjoyed under Sir Charles Norwood was gone with the formation of the corporation. So was the Company's independence. The New Zealand Motor Corporation not only produced vehicles and sold them through its dealer network, but it branched out and purchased a number of non-motor businesses. As part of a restructuring process that followed to incorporate the new businesses the organisation was in 1982 re-named EMCO Group Ltd and only three years later was purchased by Steel &Tube Ltd. The new owners soon sold off every trading arm but retained the most lucrative motor business, the NZMC Ltd. By 1991 the company decided to get out of the motor trade altogether and sold off remaining interests and stock.

A familiar name goes and a new one replaces it at the DML showroom in Courtenay Place. Photo taken on 3 November 1971. Below: End of an era—the demolition of the Norwood building, photo from 14 October 1987.

Above: Mr S.K.G. Smallbone, Managing Director of Morris Industries Exports, witnesses the signature of the largest contract for Morris cars by Walter Norwood, then General Manager of the Dominion Motors Ltd. Below: Mr C.E. Aldridge, General Sales Manager of M.I.E. and Walter Norwood inspect the 3500th Morris ordered by The Dominion Motors since 1 January 1935.

CHAPTER FOUR
Difficult Times

Many thousands of investors in the USA lost large sums of money when values of stocks and shares dropped rapidly in October 1929, the beginning of what was to be known as the Great Depression. Widespread unemployment soon followed and many people had to depend on charity or Government handouts. Begging was commonplace. Large crowds often gathered in public places to read the few job ads in displayed newspapers, while others waited outside places where jobs might be available. Unemployment was highest in inner-city working-class areas. The city was worse off than the country, men worse off than women. Workers and their families often lost their homes or could not continue renting houses. The city streets and overcrowded outskirt slums became the dwellings of the unfortunate ones, but on the other hand some Americans who kept their regular jobs during that time lived quite comfortably. Many of them still could afford to buy clothes, a car or other products.

In 1930 the Great Depression was beginning to take hold in New Zealand also. Unemployment grew high, and production was low; in other words, money did not go round. The Government encouraged people to buy locally manufactured goods and promoted slogans like "Buy New Zealand Made and Lessen Unemployment".

Dominion Motors management in the 1930s.

In addition to that, protective duties were collected on imported goods like motor-car bodies and tyres, in order to both gain revenue and contain the spending of foreign currency funds. British made car tyres for example, previously dutiable at 10 percent of value (and 40 percent from other countries), were in 1934 made subject to a duty based on the weight of the tyres! In 1927 "motor spirits" were subject to a duty of 4d per gallon; in 1930 it was increased to 6d per gallon, and increased again during 1931–32 by 2d per gallon each year.

In 1936 these protective duties were abolished on motor-car bodies, and reduced for unassembled or completely-knocked-down C.K.D car imports to encourage the local assembly of cars in New Zealand. By 1935 the economy had shown slight signs of recovery, but in 1937 the Government suddenly imposed severe import controls. A decline in overseas funds commenced during the years 1936–37, and continued steadily until 28 November 1938 when the net overseas funds of the Reserve Bank and the trading banks were under £NZ 8,000,000.

The Import Control Regulations 1938 prohibited the importation of all goods into New Zealand except under a licence, unless exemption from one was granted by the Minister of Customs. The policy generally was to ensure that after overseas debt commitments had been met from the Sterling funds, the maximum funds available would be provided for the importation of essential commodities, with particular regard to the needs of primary and industrial production.

A further important feature of the policy was the desire to give greatest possible preference to the goods of United Kingdom manufacturers, but to limit US dollar expenditure, special considerations would apply in the case of imports from dollar areas.

Over the years new vehicle sales had fallen, and as a consequence New Zealand found itself having a uneconomic and unsafe motoring fleet. To remedy the safety aspects the Warrant of Fitness Test was introduced by the Labour Government in 1937 to protect the public generally, and also second-hand car buyers from the dangers of neglected motor-vehicles. Perhaps the initial beneficiaries were Government coffers, spare parts suppliers and garages issuing the warrants.

The situation in New Zealand went from bad to worse on 1 September 1939, when World War II broke out in Europe. It took only a few days before the first economic effects were felt in far-away New Zealand. Private motoring became difficult; petrol was rationed just three days after the war declaration in order to build up the country's reserves. The allocation of petroleum fuels was calculated on a system based on the vehicles' horse power-ratings. Ration books with coupons were introduced for essential food and household items. Times were tough for most, but industry was busy producing for the "war effort". Increased production provided employment and put large sums of money back into circulation. This process happened in all countries involved, and it finally spelt the end for the decade of the Great Depression.

During the war years many trade restrictions were imposed by Government and raw materials from overseas were in short supply because of it. Motor-car assemblers like The Dominion Motors were forced to abandon vehicle production in favour of weapons and monition manufacture. The last pre-war Morris stocks were advertised as low in petrol and oil consumption and low in tyre wear. New Zealand experienced a shortage of new vehicles by 1940 and only one in six cars was less than six years old.

The early post-war years held more surprises in store for everyone and also for the motorist. Prices rose sharply, motor taxes also, and shortages in supplies of all kinds were experienced. After the economy gradually started to improve many people wanted the material comforts that they had lost, or had never owned before, including household appliances, a house and a car.

In 1950 petrol rationing was finally abolished, but during the same year the Government introduced a new obstacle for the consumer, the so called no-remittance licence system. In brief it meant that a want-to-be new car buyer had to have private funds held overseas with which to buy imported motor vehicles. Mainly this applied to those in the elite class. The Import Restrictions had been a "strait jacket" for the consumer ever since their introduction, and their abolition was frequently called for, but for the importers or manufacturers it ensured that they could sell every vehicle they imported.

In October 1951 the Minister of Customs, Mr Bowden, announced: "Next year there will be a substantial increase in the value of licences for imports of commercial vehicles, and licences for motor-cars will total slightly more than for the present year [approximately 21,000 units of which 11,500 were cars]. Final allocations for 1951 had been determined on the recommendations of the Import Advisory Committee," added the Minister. He went on to say that the import of spare parts for motor vehicles would be freed from licensing from "soft" currency sources as from 1 January next. "Because of the overseas funds position, it has not been found possible to provide for a much greater amount for licensed motor-car imports

than 1950," the Minister announced. Statements like this one were numerous in the 1950s as Governments constantly tried to adjust to the prevailing monetary conditions.

The New Zealand Government encouraged close trade links with Britain and wanted to see more British cars on the country's roads. To make this happen, it introduced protective tariffs, which made importing from Dollar areas much more expensive. The intention of these customs tariffs was, apart from obtaining revenue, the development of New Zealand's industries, the maintenance and expansion of export markets and the implementation of trade agreements. But it also restricted the car industry in providing sufficient numbers of new cars. Waiting lists grew long. By 1953 nearly 48 percent of cars were over ten years old and 12 percent were over twenty. The Motor Trade Association (MTA) lobbied for almost thirty years to have import restrictions abolished or reduced and to increase the number of cars allowed into the country. The following are selected quotes published in its monthly newsletter *The Radiator*.

"The British car manufacturers had allocated, and were willing to supply to New Zealand during 1948, more than 20,000 new motor-cars, whereas the New Zealand Government had only allocated an estimated number of 8,583 cars." (February 1948)

"…we are of the opinion, that the Government should seriously consider the question of increasing the import licences for motor-cars…" (February 1949)

"…it is significant that Australia has lifted all restrictions on imports from Great Britain." (1949)

"WE NEED MORE NEW CARS!" (March 1949)

"Insufficient cars are being imported to meet the needs of the country…"

"…an increase in import licences for motor-cars is the only solution!" (1960)

The call for more new cars continued into the early seventies, when the Government's policy was to gradually move away from import controls. On 26 February 1972 the private and commercial no-remittance import licensing schemes were finally withdrawn and the market was liberated.

CHAPTER FIVE

Richard Andrews: from Motor Engineer to Plant Manager

A native of Waihi, Richard Andrews was educated in Auckland and started work as an apprentice at G.W. Spragg Ltd, one of Auckland's pioneer motor firms. He passed the London City and Guilds examinations in Motor Engineering in 1921, and four years later left Spraggs to become Service Manager for a motor business in Wanganui. While there, he became interested in aviation and aero engines and took a course in aircraft maintenance at Sockburn, Christchurch, qualifying for a Ground Engineer's licence in 1930. At this time he was also well known in motor cycle and speedway racing events, and competed in races at both Muriwai Beach and at Henning's Speedway in a car built by the, then famous, British racing driver, Parry Thomas. On his last appearance at Henning's

Speedway he won the 1500 c.c. New Zealand Championship.

Richard Andrews first joined Dominion Motors in 1931 as Service Manager of the Wanganui branch and in 1934 he was transferred to Wellington to take charge of the Kent Terrace Service Department. Two years later, he was appointed Service Manager for all New Zealand-wide branches and towards the end of 1938 was made responsible for planning and organising the proposed Newmarket plant for the assembly of C.K.D. vehicles. This plant went into operation in 1939 producing Morris cars and commercials until the war cut off further supplies of material. Richard then returned to Wellington, where he took over the Beatty washing machine factory (a subsidiary of Dominion Motors), and a machine shop in the Thorndon building which he set up for the production of munitions and the machining of bomb casings.

Back to Auckland he came in 1946 to enlarge and re-equip the Newmarket car assembly plant to handle a greater degree of "knock down" at a higher production rate, and later in 1954, he established and organised the new commercial vehicle assembly plant at Panmure. For both plants Richard set up a simple management structure with clear lines of communication and responsibility. He was very sharp, astute, perhaps sometimes tough, but always fair. During his time in office he introduced a couple of interesting innovations under the Rehabilitation Scheme for Servicemen. War amputees and even blind people were employed and trained as machinists in the trim shop and for sub-assembly work mostly in the wiring field. He also encouraged the employment of woman

"on the line" on equal pay at a time of acute labour shortage which was regarded as a most brilliant move. Richard Andrews, in his own inimitable style kept his finger on the pulse of both plants by visiting the "floor" daily. That way he knew exactly the state of health or otherwise of the operation. Problems in the assembly industry have been many and varied since the war, but he always maintained that without the band of loyal stalwarts who shared his worries, these would have been bigger and more numerous. Richard Andrews retired at the end of December 1965, as manager of The Dominion Motors' Assembly Division in Auckland, but remained in a consultative capacity to assist with long range planning. In intervening years he was content with a little golf, fishing and cruising in comfort but he was still enthusiastic enough about motor racing to give some of his time and experience as an official at the Ardmore Grand Prix. With thoughts of safety coming before speed he looked on motor-cycling and open cars as "an expensive way of sitting in a draught."

Richard Andrews also was a member and President of the Newmarket Rotary Club. He was a superb leader.

Above: Second from left: Richard Andrews, Peter Gilberd (Editor of Motor World) *and Don Leed (Morris representative for New Zealand) introducing the Newmarket assembly plant in 1940.*
Right: Left to right: Richard Andrews (Plant Manager), Walter Norwood, Lord Nuffield, Tom Boult (New Zealand representative, Morris Industries Export), H. Mullens (Director, Morris Industries Export) and Doug Gordon (General Manager Dominion Motors Ltd) posing in front of the assembly plant that Richard Andrews helped establish (photo circa 1949).

CHAPTER SIX

Ron Stone: from Service Station Worker to Plant Manager

Ron Stone began "in the ranks" and, a warm-hearted and supremely modest man, he makes no secret of it. Ron started his working life in 1933, pumping petrol for £2 a week at one of Auckland's mid-city service stations. Across the road was a branch of Dominion Motors; he decided he'd like to try working for them, which he did.

After eight years with the Company he joined the RNZAF in 1941, later serving as a flight mechanic with the No. 6 Squadron at Tolagi, Fiji, on Catalina flying-boats. For three of the war years he worked at the RNZAF base at Hobsonville, Auckland, on the assembly of American-built Kittyhawkes. "I was doing an assembly job on aeroplanes that eventually influenced me to move into car assembly work after the war," Ron recalls.

After a five-year venture into the laundry business he rejoined Dominion Motors as a member of the planning staff in the assembly plant at Newmarket. He later became Chief Clerk and, in 1954, he was appointed Assistant Manager at the new Panmure plant. In the early 1960s, Ron Stone also became Production Supervisor and from 1962–1966 he was assistant manager for the Newmarket operations. After that he became manager of both factories.

Ron Stone's record in staff relations speaks for itself: in his time in the top seat, no major industrial problem ever arose at either the Newmarket or the Panmure plants. Dismissing the significance of this with typical modesty, he adds: "Just a bit of luck, I suppose." But those in the know put it down to more than luck.

New Zealanders who tried to knock this country's standards of car-assembly had a formidable adversary in Ron Stone. With some feeling he once said in 1971: "Don't let anyone tell you today that the standard of the English-assembled car is higher than that of vehicles assembled in this country. It simply isn't true. Of course, it may have been true in the 1950s, but it certainly isn't true now." As if to prove a point that Morrises and Austins are solidly reliable cars, Ron Stone told the interviewer that he bought a little Morris Minor in 1950 and, with his wife drove it for 120,000 miles (193,550 km). With pride he added: "23 years later we handed this car over to our daughter and she tells us it's still going strong. Not a bad record, eh?"

In July 1973 Ron Stone walked out of his office into retirement and closed the door on 32 years in the motor industry. Neville Brennan became his successor as Manager of the Newmarket car assembly plant.

CHAPTER SEVEN
The new Morris Minor

orld War II finally ended in Europe in May 1945 and in the Pacific in August 1945. Life in New Zealand slowly started to normalise again. During the six war years the car assembly industry had produced army vehicles, ammunition or other equipment for the war effort. All that was redundant now and within a short time war production machinery was removed; assembly lines were re-equipped for car manufacture, which began in May 1946, when the first C.K.D/S.K.D shipments started to arrive from Britain.

Ford introduced the Prefect, Todd Motors and Rootes Group prepared for production of Sunbeam Talbot, Humber and Hillman Cars, and General Motors built the post-war Chevrolet in 1947. The Dominion Motors' assembly plant in Newmarket started production of the Morris 8 Series E and the Morris Ten Series M cars.

New Zealand experienced a severe shortage of new cars and all manufacturers presented the market with fresh stock as soon as possible. Some bigger car producers just "blew the cobwebs" off the old pre-war designs and produced cars like the Austin Ten/Sixteen, the Vauxhall Ten and

The London Motor Show of 1952, which would have been visually similar to the 1948 one.

the Hillman Minx. In some cases small makeovers had been applied, but largely it was the old designs again.

Meanwhile in London the 35th International Motor Show was held from 18–28 October 1948 (except Sunday the 22nd) under the patronage of their Majesties the King and Queen. This event was first held in 1905 and continued each year in unbroken sequence, with exception of the periods of both wars, gaining a status unrivalled in the World's calendar of exhibitions. Manufacturers had waited nearly ten years for this event and took full advantage of it. Visitors too: over half a million people paid for admission and a substantial increase of overseas folk was

noted. The exhibition included the latest car products together with displays of motor boats, marine engines, caravans and car trailers as well as tyres and accessories and components.

Right in the middle of all this hustle and bustle the new Morris Minor had its debut, along with the Oxford — a larger brother of almost identical features and the Morris Six — the first six-cylinder car produced by Morris Motors in 10 years. The Minor range was still small, restricted only to two models, a saloon and a tourer. Both were two-door models, because its designer Alec Issigonis (later Sir Alec) initially preferred to make the car with two large doors, instead of four quite restricted openings. His aim was to give easy excess to the frequently used front seats.

The war years had caused a backlog in the car industry, which made this show busier than ever, and the Minor had to compete with an exceptional number of new models on offer.

A commentator at the time wrote: "Interest was huge, large crowds gathered at the Morris display with eyes firmly focussed on the Minors." Right from the start the car's styling appealed to the public, long before its outstanding qualities in handling and road holding became widely known. The international press later heralded the Morris Minor as the star of the show. For many Britains however a new Minor remained a dream, because nearly all early production cars were exported to comply with British Government foreign exchange earning policies. The home market had to wait not month, but years, before huge demands from the world markets could be satisfied and Minors became widely available in their home country.

On 15 February 1949, the New Zealand Motor Trade Association published this article in their newsletter, The Radiator:

"Three entirely new Morris Cars — Minor, Oxford and Six were exhibited at the Motor show, Earls Court, London, last October. Many changes have been made and innovations introduced, and the cars are now creating very considerable interest in New Zealand. Providing elbow room inside the body to an extent unparalleled in the small car field, the new 8 h.p. Morris Minor offers less resistance to the air, is no heavier than its predecessor, is faster and even more economical.

"Improved methods of packing the engine have made it possible to provide inter-axle seating, yet the Minor gives 5 to 6 inches more leg room front and rear than in the Morris 8 E, 3 inches more usable width, and 4 inches greater width over the rear seat without appreciably increasing the length over that of the old Eight.

"The exceptional body width of the Minor means the adoption of unusual proportions of track to wheelbase (50 5/16 and 86 inches respectively) which in conjunction with the independent front wheel torsion bar suspension provides road-holding and general stability never before achieved in a car of this horsepower. Rack and pinion steering gives perfect steering geometry, reducing tyre wear since the front wheels are not artificially steered over bumps and irregularities. These wheels are also arranged to swivel through a very wide angle, giving a smaller turning circle and greater control.

"All the steel metal front of the Minor, except the wings forms the bonnet of the car and when lifted, discloses the entire power unit and accessories, so that groping for the dipstick and similar 'blind' operations are abolished. An additional refinement in the field of low-priced cars is the provision of automatic under-bonnet

illumination when the parking lights are on. As in the Oxford and Six provision is made for the simple and rapid installation of radio and heater."

The Nuffield Exports Statistics document the dispatch of two units of fully built up 2-door MM's to Dominion Motors in 1948, which arrived in New Zealand early in 1949 when Dominion Motors started preparations for the assembly of the Minor (and Oxford). These two cars were Pilot models used by Dominion Motors' engineers as a blue print for the assembly from C.K.D. A first large shipment of 1734 units was dispatched later the same year and from then on for the next twenty years they kept coming and coming... New Zealand had its Morris Minor!

CHAPTER EIGHT

The Newmarket Assembly Division 1939–1978

When you walk around the busy up-market shopping streets of Central Auckland's Newmarket district today, you do not expect to find, tucked away in one of the less glamorous side streets just off the main Broadway a large concrete building that once was a busy car factory. It looks distinctively different compared to all the modern glass palaces that now dominate the area.

The parcel of land containing one acre, two roods, twenty perches was purchased by The Dominion Motors Limited on 17 October 1938, when the landscape there was very much greener. The neighbourhood was made up from Victorian villas dotted around on the hillside and a mix of industrial and retail businesses as well as working class homes on small sections situated on the lower levels. By today's standards it was a small car factory constructed with concrete walls, covered with a saw-tooth type roof supported by wooden and steel trusses and vertical steel pillars. The main production area was at ground level but there also was a mezzanine floor at the front of the building for administration offices and trim manufacturing workshops.

Now over 50 years on, the building appears externally unchanged; yes it has new aluminium framed glass doors where the old roll gates used to be and it had a new coat of paint in 2000, but largely the outside facade is left unchanged, even the big concrete lettering on top of the front fascia wall, reading "The Dominion Motors" is proudly displayed again, after being boarded up for some

A view of the Newmarket assembly plant taken ca 1949/50

Left: A photo taken in 1949. From left: Richard Andrews (Plant Manager), Mr H. Mullens (Morris Exports) Tom Boult (Morris Exports, NZ), Doug Gordon (DML General Manager), Walter Norwood and Lord Nuffield. Below left: The same spot, 52 years later.

Customers enjoy Café Extreme's hospitality where once thousands of assembled cars left the factory.

time in recent years. The 70,000 square foot floor space is now subdivided for a small number of retail businesses and a very classy café which is well-known beyond Auckland's Bombay Hills, the metropolitan "border" in the south.

Apart from the now redundant 5-ton crane, once used to unload thousands of C.K.D. arrivals, all other evidence of the plant's car making days is gone.

The author travelled several times to the site to gather the information for this story, but when he first arrived there it was night time, the doors were already shut for business and everyone had gone. The hustle and bustle of the day had given

way to relative tranquillity again. He walked around for a while in front of the building that is the birthplace of most Morris Minor Saloons built in New Zealand. He took in the atmosphere, perhaps feeling similar to how a pilgrim would on a visit to Mecca or similar holy places. He paused for some time at the gate where thousands of Morris Minors had left the factory to be taken on their 2 mile test drive through town, as it was in those days. Thoughts of

Trim manufacture at Newmarket during the early years of Morris Minor production. Above, the so-called wood shop where the plywood head-liners and luggage shelves for the MMs and Oxfords were made. Below, the upholstery workshop which was situated on the mezzanine floor at the front of the building.

Left: One of many thousands—a crate of Morris Minor parts ready to be collected by the transport contractor, A.B. Wrights. Below: Arrival in the assembly plant.

inventing a time machine crossed his mind while he was pressing his nose against the glass door, somehow expecting to see a glimpse of the last Morries rolling off the line, but there was no such luck. The reality was the interior of a modern shopping complex, illuminated by halogen spot lights. Oh...yes, there were some cars on display, as prizes for a lottery, but unfortunately of the brand with the star, not the bull.

Through another glass door the author saw tables and chairs stacked, belonging to Café Extreme, where well-to-do white collar members of society would gather the next morning for a pre-office chat and a first dose of caffeine to kick-start the day. He wondered if they had any idea that right behind the coffee bar fifty-odd years ago a massive hydraulic hoist pushed out of the concrete floor lifting the brand-new shiny cars for their final inspection? Probably not.

The factory, established by Sir Walter Norwood and masterminded by Richard Andrews, opened in 1939 as a then modern car assembly plant, designed to produce vehicles from C.K.D. imports. By the late 1940s an estimated seventy people worked here, a number that gradually built up as the Company and the demand for cars grew in New Zealand. At its peak of production in the 1970s were some 400 workers on the floor.

From the start of production, Mr Richard Andrews was the Manager, assisted by three others: Thomas Sefton Finch (Accountant), Maurice E. Coates (Factory Supervisor), and

Colin L. Thompson, (Technical Supervisor).

From the very beginning Richard Andrews set up a very simple, but clear-cut management structure with crystal clear lines of communication, authority and responsibility, with no academic middle management required. Some say he "ran a very tight ship." Andrews himself received instructions directly from Sir Charles or Sir Walter, both based in Wellington, but in this factory his orders concerning the day-to-day operations were the undisputed law; he was truly in charge of the whole thing.

Soon after the factory first opened, World War II broke out in Europe and civilian car production was put on hold in order to produce for the "war effort". In 1945 when the situation slowly normalised again and the plant re-started production with some S.K.D. Morris commercial vehicles. But soon after the Morris Series E and M10 were imported as C.K.D. packs. They were built here until in 1949 preparations started for

Above: A small crate containing Morris Minor body parts is uncased.

Right: In preparation for assembly panels are degreased in flat tanks.

assembly of the brand new Morris Minor Series MM as well as the Oxford, which both had been introduced in London's Earls Court one year earlier. Two pilot cars arrived prior to first C.K.D. shipments later that year. From then on assignments became regular and crates were delivered by truck from the wharf to the factory's back gate unloaded by a heavy crane or forklift and piled up four or five high along the back wall. This area was known as the unpacking bay. They were stored here until orders from Head Office required stocks to be released into production. The person in charge of C.K.D and Stores received advanced packing lists which itemised the contents of each crate which was then sorted into a departmental order. Panels were taken to the degreasing troughs in the body-shop and stacked next to them. Degreasing was

Morris Minor floor pans arrived pre-assembled ready to mount onto the jig base. Here workers prepare for the body assembly.

Below left: Dominion Motors engineers made their own jigs, here used to support the body in construction.

in the beginning a dirty manual operation, later being replaced by a semi-automated process, first of its kind in NZ, invented and built by Technical Supervisor, Colin Thompson. In this process the oil that had been applied prior to exporting as a rust protective coatingwas removed. Clean panels were taken to storage shelves or simply stacked on the floor in the body-shop, always in close proximity to the section that required them.

Mechanical components, such as engine-gearbox units, running gear and suspension parts were stored on stands along the assembly track. Engines arrived here without some of their auxiliary components fitted, items like that were attached "off- line" and units stored here until required.

But not all vehicle components were imported from the UK because of New Zealand

Government legislation designed to preserve Sterling funds and to develop a home-grown industry. Locally based firms, often branches of the English mother firm, manufactured many components that were needed to make the cars, and that way provided New Zealanders with work and income, a policy that seems totally foreign to present day politicians. Some of the major contributors were Dunlop for tyres, British Australian Lead Manufacturers B.A.L.M. (later ICI) for Paint, Lucas NZ for Electrical items, and in later years Pilkington for windscreen glass.

The majority of the plant's operations were "on the line" assembling of the cars, but it also had off-line assembly or manufacture workshops such as trim manufacture upstairs and the tiny wood shop tucked away in a corner. In these areas worked about 12–14 people making upholstery for the seats and all other items such as interior liners, head liners and the carpets. Other sub-assembly areas made the wiring looms, pre-assembled front suspensions or completed the engine-gearbox units, to name just a few.

These off-line operations employed a number of returned service people of whom some had sustained severe war injuries. Blind persons were engaged in the making of, for example, the wiring looms. This was made possible through a well-organised operation in which the blind operator could be trained to follow a set pattern routinely.

Women worked off-line too where the tasks were regarded as physically less demanding; in sections such as the mechanical sub-assembly and in the wet-deck area of the paint shop. But a small number of them were to be found "on the line" in final trim and one is remembered to have worked in the body-shop, physically the most demanding section of all. We must not forget these were the years of labour shortage and there was more work to do than there were people available to do it.

Of course a few women also worked in the more traditional jobs in the offices. The days before the modern photocopiers required many typists, and this factory had about four of them in the early 1950s.

The Body-Shop

The making of a car such as the Morris Minor started in the body-shop where the body shells were built-up. The expression C.K.D. (Completely Knocked Down) to describe the way these cars were imported, it is strictly speaking not correct, because they were *not* completely knocked down. The assembly of the cars' floor pan was a delicate operation which required very accurate jigging. It determined the wheelbase, the track width and gave important reference to the construction of the upper body. This work was already done at Nuffield's, the exporter, where they had the required equipment.

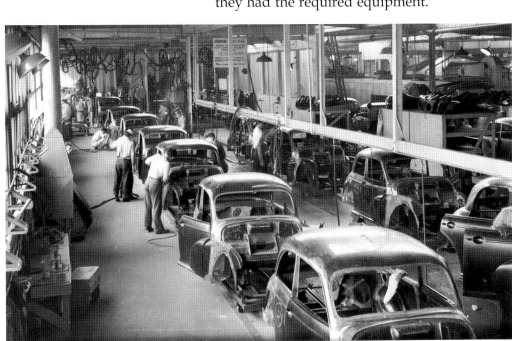

The Morris Minor two-door line on the left and the four-door line on the right. Often the Minors were all assembled in one line and the other was for the Oxfords.

This photo from the early 1960s shows at left the end of the body shop assembly line and at right a body being hoisted into the phosphating machine. In the centre a Wolseley 6/99 body has reached the end of the line.

Floor pan units covered everything from the front bumper studs to the lower boot floor panel in the rear. They came pre-assembled with inner sills, boxing plates, chassis legs, toe board panels, inner front wheel arch panels and the shock absorber mounting cross member. Virtually the complete underframe of the car came out of the box. The whole unit was placed onto a jig base, a very heavy sturdy steel frame, similar to a short legged table. Pedestals with brackets and heavy clamps had been bolted to the level surface of the base, providing reliable points of reference. Strong clamps held the floor pan firmly in place for assembly of all upper body parts. That way only smaller portable jigs and brackets were needed to determine the correct position for the door hinge pillars (A posts) and side panels (B posts). Often smaller, less important panels did not need jigging at all, their shape already determined their correct fit and position for others, such as the dashboard or the roof skin. All panels arrived coated in a black primer, which had to be removed in areas that required spot welding to allow fusion. Overlapping panels were temporarily held in place by clamps until spot welding was completed. When the body shell was assembled in its basic form, the doors were hung and adjusted to the required clearances using a jig. After completion of this

stage the body was given a production number tag and hoisted onto a flat trolley run on four swivel castor wheels. Support brackets on both ends of the trolley engaged into the arched under frame at the rear and the front chassis legs of the body.

The whole unit was to be manually pushed along a U-channel track further down the line. As a next step in the operation unwanted seams were filled with body solder and worked back to a smooth finish. Workers with the title of 'Line Charge Hand' checked the body panels for any small blemishes and marked them with chalk for rectification, panel beating or polishing what ever the case might have been.

The front guards were also designated to the body and loosely attached, but spaced away from the inner flitch panel with a cross bar at radiator level and smaller flat bar brackets attached to the front jacking point. Bonnet and boot lid were offered up temporarily using so called dummy hinges with thumbscrews to hold them, they allowed propping up of the panel. All this was necessary to give the spray painters free access to all areas of the body-shell without having to touch any of it during the paint process. From here on the completed shell left the body shop and travelled along the track into the paint-shop area.

The Paint-Shop and Phosphate Application

A fundamental principle of a good and lasting paint job is the thorough preparation of the surface its going on, which has to be clean and free from all traces of grease. The newly arrived body-shells were everything but exactly that. Therefore the first step in the operation was an Alkali Cleaner treatment applied through a steam lance for two minutes at 50°C. In this process dust, chalk, gas welding oxide, finger marks and black primer were removed, which left the panels bare and clean. In a second step the steel surface received a coating of Iron Posphate through the application of an I.C.I product called Duridine, again applied by steam lance for 3-5 minutes at 60 °C, which acted as a rust inhibitor.

From 1956 onwards the Newmarket plant operated an initial anti-corrosion treatment which was marketed under the slogan of "A dip in time saves...rust." Engineers built a big tank containing 1,300 gallons of the rust inhibitor Duridine which was formulated to create a kind of tough, second skin on the steel body. The motor bodies, carried by an overhead conveyor, were dipped into the inhibitor almost up to the window line and left submerged for some minutes, then lifted clear of the tank for operators to wipe away further excess of the black liquid to prevent runs from forming and marking the finish. Included in the dipping process was the use of special guns which flooded body compartments above the dip level with inhibitor liquid. The plant's technical adviser, Colin Thompson, once put on record: "There are a number of points in a car body that just cannot be reached by ordinary spraying. The only way of getting a proper job done is to dip the body and leave the inhibitor to soak its way right through. There is not a corrosion-prone point in the car which is not reached by this dip-and-spray treatment." The black liquid which provided the first protective coating on the car was followed by two more coats of inhibitor before the first was allowed to dry (top left, page 60).

Now the car body was fully prepared for the DUCO paint system. The primer used, lacquer based, was a highly pigmented primer which was sprayed on and then baked in a chambre at

Above: A body has been pushed into the primer spray booth. Below: Primed bodies enter the top coat spray booth. Here can be seen clearly how guards, bonnet and boot lid were allocated to the body, but temporarily held by brackets.

130–150°C for 30 minutes. The body shell was advanced to the so called wet deck and allowed to cool down. Here all visually important outside areas were sanded down manually with fine

After the top coat was baked and cooled down the paint surface had to be cut and buffed to achieve the required finish. This was a very delicate operation, which needed a light hand but lots of stamina.

The revolving jig, the first stage of the chassis line. Just one man could turn a car over with ease. In the background are chassis and large engines for the assembly of Morris Commercials.

emery paper and water, to achieve maximum adhesion of the top coat and smoothness of the surface. The bodies were allowed to dry and later wiped with so called "tack-rags", a type of cheese cloth impregnated with an adhesive substance to attract and hold dust particles.

Immediately after preparations were completed the car body was wheeled into the paint spray booth to receive the top coat. In the early days of Minor production the colour range was very limited. Some of them were: Belmont Green, Epsom Beige and Duck Egg Blue. Some years later Snow White and a larger selection of colours were on offer. (Customers usually did

not care too much as long as they got a car.) A nitrocellulose lacquer was sprayed with 6 double header coats and could be air dried, but Dominion Motors' assembly operation engaged a heated drying booth to force dry the paint film at 25–30°C for about 30 minutes. After the coating had cooled down the surface was "cut" and polished using Dulux cutting and polishing pastes. Electric buffs with lambs wool pads were used for this task which required skilled operators and extreme care, as the new paint film could easily be damaged.

During the years of Morris Minor production, many modifications were made to the car itself,

Here a worker at each end fits running gear. The pedestals were padded on the outside to prevent paint damage.

and to the assembly methods including the paint systems. The nitrocellulose lacquers were found to be prone to chalking and chipping, especially noticeable under New Zealand's high ultra-violet levels. As technology progressed Dulux offered from about 1960 onwards a new top coat system. An alkyd primer was sprayed and baked at 150°C for 30 minutes and afterwards rubbed down to a smooth finish. Two top coats of an alkyd baking enamel were applied and the solvent allowed to migrate out of the paint film which was then baked at 220°C for 30 minutes.

In 1965 Dominion Motors made a change to a blend of acrylic and alkyd paints. Two coats were

Another car is ready to be lifted back on the trolley to have the engine gearbox unit fitted. In the background are stacks of CKD supplies and preassembled engine/gearbox units.

applied and baked for 30 minutes at 220°C. This coating gave a gloss finish off the gun without having to polish. Its most important advantage for the customer was the improved quality; the paint did not chalk or chip the same as the Alkyd or Nitrocellulose lacquers did.

Some time during the 1970s ICI replaced their product DURIDINE (iron phosphate) with zinc phosphate which provided much greater rust prevention from the start. (A shame that it was too late for Morris Minors!)

But back to the early days: after completion of buffing and polishing the car bodies were advanced on their trolleys into the so called final-line where dozens of smaller items were fitted. The exact sequence of operation in this area could not be traced, but it began with the proper fitting of front and rear guards. Fairly early in the process the radiator grille was offered up, supplied off-line with headlights and all trimmings. (This too changed with the introduction of the Series II models). Bonnet and boot lids were taken off their dummy hinges. Only the boot lid was fitted with chromed hinges while the bonnet was taken to shelves near the final-trim line where they would re-join their allocated car later.

Somewhere in the middle of this assembly process the wiring loom and other electrical components such as regulator, petrol pump and windscreen wiper found their homes followed by outer door lock handles, door lock mechanisms and striker plates. The list goes on, but the last operation in this line was the fitting of nearly all window glass with exception of the door windows and their channels.

From here on the car bodies left the track of the assembly track and were side lined in a holding area before entering the mechanical line. But work did not stop here, the petrol tank and smaller bits and pieces in the engine bay were installed such as the front Armstrong shock absorbers.

The Chassis-Line / Mechanical Line

Up to this point the cars-to-be had no suspensions or running gear fitted. Work on that began in the roll-over-jig, a steel construction not unlike a spit roast, that made it possible to rotate the car body upside down. Jig adaptor brackets were bolted to the front bumper studs and the rear floor panel. (This arrangement changed with the introduction of rear bumper studs in 1951.) Two padded claws were hooked under the roof reinforcement panels of both door openings and connected to a strong cross beam over the roof in which the hoist engaged. The body shell was lifted off its trolley and carefully lowered into this jig, and secured. One of the jig's two revolving heads was low geared and had to be operated by crank. This allowed the car body to be turned upside down safely and reasonably effortlessly by one man.

Up to four workers, each one responsible for his own quarter of the cars' underside, then set out to fit mechanical components. Each had his own pedestal which acted as a work bench for

The end of the mechanical line. Last job—road wheels on—and down the ramp it goes!

Top: The right lane is going to the mechanical assembly, the left lane is leaving it. In the right background is the paint shop. Below: A view taken from the opposite angle. The bicycles belong to workers without cars. Insert: The space today is occupied by a furniture showroom.

Another contrast of then and now. The best points of reference for comparison are the windows and roller door—these features have not altered much.

tools, boxes of fasteners, and also as a work platform elevated two feet off the floor for easier access. One side facing the car was padded to protect panel and paints. The rear axle with leaf spring was assembled off side and dropped into place with help of the electric hoist mentioned earlier. Front suspensions were also pre-assembled by the workers during car change over times, and later installed as complete units. At this point of the operation the cardan shaft, exhaust system and fuel/brake lines were installed. After completion of these tasks, the car was righted again and lifted on to the elevated track, off the Chassis-line, this time supported by two small trolleys, one front and one aft.

As a final step in the mechanical assembly process the engine-gearbox units were lowered-

in and secured, the radiator was fitted and all connections made. A few last jobs in this section included the fitting of the steering wheel, the adjustment of the handbrake cables, oiling and greasing, and finally the fitting of road wheels. After completion of it all the handbrake was applied and the car given a push down the sloping end of the track until it stopped by itself sitting on its own wheels for the first time, ready to enter the next stage of assembly.

The Final Trim Line

The cars were pushed a short distance across from the end of the chassis-line into the final trim line where work on them continued with the fitting of draught excluders around the doorsills and boot, followed by both bumpers, the plywood luggage shelf, the bonnet, the ventilator-glass channel assembly of the doors, the carpets, fascia shelf and all interior liners, and finally the seats. At the end of the line the vehicles had a battery installed, were given a small amount of petrol ready for a first start up and a strict final inspection.

The Final Inspection Department

At the end of the final trim line was a small area set aside for inspection, testing and minor rectification. It was a relatively simple process then, compared to today's hi-tech approach.

They had no electronic performance analysis and not even a brake tester as we know it today, just a hydraulic hoist, and two miles of city streets.

Tim Bell, the Chief Inspector, an ex-Air Force man with excellent technical knowledge, reliability and reputation, was in charge of this department. Newly completed vehicles were initially hoisted up and all functions tested; if found to be faulty they were either corrected on the spot, or serious rejects were sent back to the section in which the problem had occurred. Small paint damage was dealt with in the touch up area next to the hoist, and again, bigger problems were referred back to the spray painters.

Only after the visual inspection was successfully completed and the vehicle had passed, was it then driven by Tim Bell's Road Test Inspectors onto public roads and tested for brake, steering functions and so on. Cars that had been given the final "nod" were parked on the concrete area just at the front of the factory and had to be taken back inside at the end of each shift, until they were dispatched. This probably was acceptable during the 1940s when output was relatively small, but as the production

Top: Early days—every night the completed vehicles had to be taken back inside until they were delivered.
Above: Conditions started to improve after 1956 when the storage yard was created at the back of the plant.

volume increased during the 1950s footpath storage space ran out. A section of adjoining residential property was purchased in January 1956 and made into a small new car yard.

Achievements

During some 40 production years the following Morris/BMC passenger car models were produced in this plant: the Morris 8 Series E and 10 Series M, the Morris Minor Series MM, Series II and 1000, the Morris Oxford M O, Series V and Series VI, M.G. Magnette Mark IV, the Morris Six and Isis, the Mini Minor (later called Mini), the Wolseley Hornet and 6/99, the Morris/Austin/Wolseley/Riley/MG 1100/1300 models, the Morris 1800, the Morris Marina, the Allegro, the Morris Kimberley and Tasman, the Leyland P76. The years prior to 1954 included also the following commercials: the Morris-Commercial 5cwt , the Morris J Van 10-12cwt (Town Express), the Morris-Commercial 5 ton (Petrol & Diesel). In 1978 it was decided to centralise all Auckland production into the Panmure plant and close the Newmarket operations by Christmas that year.

Recent Developments

On 26 June 1980 the New Zealand Post Office purchased the building for workshops from the New Zealand Motor Corporation (prior to its formation, The Dominion Motors Limited) for $1,120,000. Telecom Auckland Limited took over the property on 13 February 1990 after Telecom had been set up as a State-Owned Enterprise by the Crown, but Telecom then on-sold it to Millpark Properties Limited on 8 August 1993. Since 2 June 1999 the building has been owned by Auckland One Limited, a property company which, subject to resource consent, plans to demolish the building and re-develop the site into a modern shopping complex by 2003. While the author wishes them business success, he quietly hopes that this landmark, this remainder of a once proud New Zealand car industry, will survive.

Morris Minor 1000 production at the Newmarket plant during the early 1960s. Note the Mini above the DURIDINE tank

CHAPTER NINE

Eric Ludlow: from Assembly Worker to C.K.D. Supervisor

Eric started work for DML in the Newmarket Assembly Plant in early 1947, when there were about 70 people there inclusive of management. Many of them were ex-service people out of the Army, Navy and Airforce. He says there were quite a few characters there, but they got on well and it was a good crowd to work with.

The Assembly Division's Manager was Richard Andrews, a down-to-earth and straight thinking man who was solely in charge of the whole operation, assisted by T.S. Finch in Accounts, Maurice Coates ("Morrie") as Production Supervisor and Colin Thompson, the Engineers Officer.

Eric's first job there was "on the line" in the electrical section installing the wiring on the Morris Series 10 M and Series 8 E models which had been in production again since the end of the war.

In those days it was only a small team compared to later years; they had to be multifunctional as it is termed today, and when vehicles had to be delivered to the wharf or rail yard, the dispatch officer rounded up a few assembly workers to drive them. So Eric was dragged away from the line quite often, which always was a very welcome change from the repetitive assembly work.

He recalls that early in 1949 they heard rumours about some revolutionary new Morris cars due to arrive soon in New Zealand. They arrived not long after; an Oxford MO and a Minor MM. They were both fully built up cars shipped from England to the Port of Wellington and unpacked there for Head Office, because their top management wanted to have a good look at them before they were sent up by rail to

Auckland. Roley Chaplyn was in charge of dispatch; he and Eric were asked to pick up these two cars and drive them back to the Assembly Plant in Newmarket right in the heart of Auckland, as it was then.

They were transported on a flat deck wagon, open, but covered up with rail covers. Once they were slung off, they had to be removed from the scene very quickly! The instructions that had been given were not to let anyone see too much and keep moving. Roley drove the Oxford and Eric took the Minor, a what later became known as a low-lite model, in a khaki colour. "It was quite a historical moment, really, when I think of it, being the first Morris Minor driver in New Zealand."

The Minor was the latest thing out in those days after the old Morris Series E and M 10 and drew a lot of attention from the public who spotted them being driven along the city streets. Both cars were used as pilot-models and had been made not long after production started at Cowley 1948. "They were still in need of some

Morris 8, Series E assembly at Newmarket in the late 1940s.

attention to detail, for example on the Minor, the door sealing rubbers," he remembers, "kept falling off every time you opened the door—thick round rubbers glued onto the edge of the door sills, but soon after our production started later that year, they were replaced with the clip-on draught excluder as we knew them ever since."

They got the cars back to the plant "under cover" as best as possible given the circumstances. Soon after, Chief Engineer Colin Thompson and his team descended on them, dismantled them completely, and took measurements of all key points for the fabrication of DML's own production jigs needed in the assembly process from C.K.D. Many months after that the cars were re-assembled and they used the Minor as a company runabout for a very long time, mainly forth and back to the rail and wharf offices. "The Oxford had a better life, it became Richard Andrews' car which he kept for nearly six years 'till the new Oxford came out in '55," he believes.

Meanwhile Eric continued working on the line in the electrical section and eventually worked on the first of the Minors, installing the wiring-

loom, feeding it through the body, connecting the junction box, fuel pump, lights and the like.

One day the boss of the dispatch department, Roley Chaplyn, asked him to come and work in his section permanently. That was all right, Eric loved the idea and soon moved from wiring to dispatch where he spent the next three years. Eric's duties involved arranging suitable transport for the Company's products according to the delivery information sent to them from Head Office in Wellington. They requested the quantity of cars and the destination of each, even quoted the production number and the details of the future owner. According to this information they marked the vehicles with a destination sticker on the windscreen and placed it on stand-by for dispatch.

It was Eric's daily job to go down to the rail yard to see what was available in terms of wagons. "If you just phoned them they would not tell you what they had—you had to be there in person and ask them nicely." Often, for example, the conversation that followed was like this: Eric: "What can I have today?" Rail: "We've got a couple of UBs and one U and an M". Eric:

The collier Kaimai *seen leaving Auckland for Westport or Greymouth, its deck cargo consisting of Morris Minors and one Volkswagen. Below: The photo of the* Kaimai *was taken by Clifford W. Hawkins, seen with his family on a holiday in Northland boiling the "billy". Naturally they travelled by Morris Minor.*

"Can I have them?" Rail: "Well, maybe..". Eric: "I need them urgently!" Rail: "All right then!"

Eric would phone back to the office and tell Roley what he had scored for now. By the time he got back to the plant he had rounded up the other drivers, collected the keys from the office and stuck the six D-plates on ("that's all we had"), and away they went.

"I can say in all fairness the people I dealt with from NZR were good guys, they helped wherever they possibly could, I never had any real nastiness at all. But having said that, it all depended on who the guys were and how you approached them. Generally the blokes in charge there were good, but if they told you that you could not have what you wanted—that was the final word in the matter; you didn't argue!" In those days New Zealand Railways had a monopoly on long distance land transport "and they knew how to use it."

Once the vehicles were loaded onto the wagons, DML workers were not allowed to touch them anymore; strict union rules protected railway jobs. Rail staff took over securing them with thick hemp rope and covering up with heavy tarpaulins. "Quite frankly they did such a lot of damage, that in the end we had to supply special soft covers to protect the paintwork first." This method worked very well for the paintwork, but getting the covers returned from the dealers didn't work so well.

All vehicles destined for the South Island markets went on coastal freighters mostly operated by the Union Steamship Company. Those vessels were colliers designed to sail in shallow waters, and they could hold cars inside as well as on deck.

Eric had to ring the port office to find out when such a boat was due in, and remain on stand by until it actually birthed. "Then it was all hands on deck, we had to get the drivers together to

Above: The collier Kaitangata *laden with Morris Minors and destined for South Island customers.*
Right: Another shipment of Minors and an Oxford arrived at Westport and awaiting distribution to dealers.

take the vehicles down to port. Some times we were shifting cars all day, especially when we took them to the boats. For our return transport we often used the store's truck."

One day they had to go down to Auckland wharf and deliver a shipload of MO Oxfords. The skipper of this particular vessel had had a fire on board of one of his previous boats loaded with cars, and he was so paranoid about it that he would not accept the cargo unless they disconnected every single battery. "None of us was too impressed with that; it made our jobs so much harder, but we had a lot of 'fun' with that one. Cars were slung on to the boat then, not roll-on roll-off like these days, and similar union rules applied here so we were not allowed to drive them onto the slings — that had to be done by a wharfie! But we watched them closely!"

Regardless of union rules they had to go down into the holds and assist with the lowering down of vehicles, and pushing them until the loading officer in charge was happy with the final position. Only then were they allowed to apply the hand brake and lock the doors. "Usually two of us got roped into that...oh, it was a sod of a job, because these ships were also used to cart West Coast coal on their return to Auckland. After a day's work down there we were absolutely filthy, covered in coal dust, and so

were the cars on arrival, but it did not concern us too much, we had done our bit, it was now over to the dealers to make them presentable."

During this stage of Eric's life his family came along. He realised there wasn't enough money in the dispatch work, so after some soul-searching he suggested to the boss that he had to have a job that paid more or he would look elsewhere for employment. "He offered me charge of the fork hoist and the heavy cranes in the unpacking bay, after all it was worth an extra ten 'bob' a week, which made a big difference in those days. I did this job until the new Assembly Plant in Panmure was built in 1953 and that year three of us worked there helping to build the equipment."

They were involved in the making of the assembly lines, the tracks, the shelving, the paint booths and the paint baking ovens. Things had to be built from scratch; he remembers the ovens: they were made from large sheets of metal formed into a double wall panel and filled with Vermicalite as a thermal insulator. "When the

*Early days in Panmure. Below: An aerial shot from 1954 and at bottom another from 1957. C.K.D. storage is still in the open air.
Right: "Brutus" the log hauler in action.*

Panmure plant commenced production in '54, I left my previous position in Newmarket and became in charge of the C.K.D stocks and stores. This involved driving the loader in the yard, a converted log hauler, we named *Brutus;* it was the first machine we had out there to do the heavy lifting of C.K.D packs, but later we had a Yale fork hoist. In the early years of the Panmure plant, say '54 to beginning of '58 we had no shelter whatsoever for the crates, they were delivered in from the wharf by A.B.Wrights, a transport contractor, and stacked outside three or four high, depending on their height and weight. In our yard we also looked after Newmarket's C.K.D stocks but clearly separated

Above and right: Morris Minor C.K.D. as it was packed at Morris Industries Exports. One notes the assembled floor pans.
Below: Uncasing of what looks like Morris Mini parts.

from ours. The slightest mix up would have made a search for a stray pack quite time consuming."

In the heydays of production of Minis, Morris 1100/1300s and the Minor Vans, not to mention the vast range of heavy commercial vehicles, they would have some 2500 cases in stock, which on average guaranteed production for both assembly plants for six months.

The cases were quite primitive — simple boxes nailed together from rough sawn timber. Some of their roof tops were not weather-proof at all, so they had to cover them up with plastic sheets to protect them from the weather, particularly in winter. Every one of the crates had a series of numbers and information stencilled onto its sides, like Nuffield's logo and the destination

DM–Auckland. The crate's external measurements were given, also the weight, for example GROSS 37 CWTS, and some indication of the main content, such as Morris Minor roof tops, trimmings or engines of which the engine-numbers were also listed. But the most relevant information were the code numbers at the very end in the top corner of each case, they would relate to a more detailed shipping list received in advance from Head Office. "According to production orders given by them we had to find the required packs to make up all components for x-number of cars, and move into the unpacking bay. The yard was not tarsealed at all, just rolled down clay which caused us a lot of hassle during the wet season, we'd be slipping

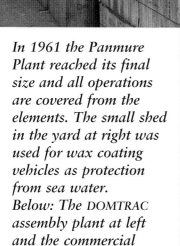

In 1961 the Panmure Plant reached its final size and all operations are covered from the elements. The small shed in the yard at right was used for wax coating vehicles as protection from sea water.
Below: The DOMTRAC *assembly plant at left and the commercial assembly plant at right.*

particularly the ones with running gear in them, which was always secured at the base of the box. Usually six engine-gearbox units were packed, three on each end for even weight distribution. The fork hoist driver had to be very careful when lifting them off a high stack. Normally the packing staff at Nuffield's would correctly indicate with a marking on the pack where the centre of gravity lay, but one could never be absolutely certain about that. "Sometimes they gave us wrong directions, well... we found that out the hard way when the driver picked up a case supposedly correct, but the whole thing went... ouch!"

On top of the base layer made up from running gear, springs, all heavy items, were the other bits and pieces like panels stacked onto each other, doors, guards, and floor pans. Smaller gaps between it all were stuffed with rims or starter motors, generators, carburettors and distributors. The inside walls of the cases were lined with thick paper for extra protection and all steel panels were coated in a white oil, called press oil. To limit the movement of parts during shipping everything was tightly packed and for additional safety tied together with heavy duty twine. It seems hilarious today, but it was quite adequate and transport damage was very limited.

and sliding around — oh, it was a real mud pile at times. In the summer the opposite: the wind was blowing the dust around — you just could not win. Conditions improved a lot for us in '58 when a new C.K.D storage building was completed and put into service. It was higher than the older buildings to accommodate the tower of the new fork lift. The fact that the shed had a concrete floor and also kept the rain out made our jobs so much more comfortable, but we still had to get across the open space between the buildings until 1961 when a third building was erected to bridge the gap."

The wooden cases were quite heavy,

After unpacking, the panels were taken to the de-greasing bay to be washed down manually in large flat tanks and then moved on trolleys to the store or sometimes directly to the body shop and stacked near the jigs, ready to be used. Engines etc. were taken to a mechanical sub-assembly area to have all auxiliary components fitted, ready to be dropped into the cars at the chassis line.

"Frequent industrial action by the wharfies occurred and our contractor could not uplift new

DECK CARGO SUFFERS WHEN . . .

CYCLONE STRIKES DUTCH FREIGHTER

WITH some wrecked motor-cars scattered about on her decks and shattered car parts tangled up with her winches and hanging at crazy angles from the split and broken cases on her decks, the Dutch freighter Amstelveen (7148 tons gross) arrived at Wellington on Saturday afternoon a week overdue from London after striking a fierce Pacific cyclone.

Scarred and rust-covered after a continuous battering from giant seas almost all the way from Panama to Wellington, the Amstelveen herself had fittings torn from the outsides of her after deckhouses.

The many shattered cases of rusting car parts among the Amstelveen's badly-damaged deck cargo were a depressing sight for representatives of motor-car companies who went down to the ship at the Queen's Wharf early this morning to inspect the wreckage.

It will not be known whether cargo in the Amstelveen's holds has been damaged until she is unloaded. Even cases six feet high and many times longer, which were secured to the ship's more-sheltered aft hatch covers, were pushed over to one side of her decks by the impact of the heavy seas.

Naturally it was too dangerous for the Amstelveen's crew to unlash and relash her deck cargo during any part of her stormy Pacific crossing, so the battered cases of car parts were strengthened simply by more and more wire-spring ropes being wound around those that had moved from their anchorings.

Waves Over Bridge

Describing the Amstelveen's ordeal, the steward (Mr. A. N. Ancher) said that waves washed right over the top of her bridge. Five motor

car wheels and tyres which escaped from one case when the huge seas broke it open, careered around the decks until members of the crew captured them and put them in one of the ship's lockers. The wheels were still in the lockers this morning.

Mr. Ancher said that as far as he knew no cargo was lost overboard. Although the Amstelveen was badly tossed around in the Pacific, her voyage was not as bad as the one she made from Halifax to Holland at the same time as the Flying Enterprise epic was taking place in the Atlantic. Mr. Ancher pointed to deckhouses, cabin doors, portholes, and superstructure which had been stove-in on that voyage and which had since been repaired. He said the Amstelveen put back 200 miles to escape the worst of the storm which caught the Flying Enterprise.

The Amstelveen's master (Captain H. Bennink) was ashore this morning, Dominion Motors, Ltd., alone had a consignment of 60 cars on the ship, said the branch manager (Mr. J. M. Brough). Among these were 26 convertibles like that pictured above as virtually wrecked. The Amstelveen is under charter to the N.Z. Shipping Co.

"HAVING a reputation for being funny can be rather a heavy load to carry and my heart sank like a stone the other day when I went to open a bazaar and a kindly-intentioned lady met me at the door and said; 'You will make us laugh, won't you?' "—Joyce Grenfell, the well-known comedienne speaking in a B.B.C. programme for women

GIANT WAVES WRECK CARS ON SHIP'S DECK

Two seamen on the Dutch freighter Amstelveen, now in Wellington, look at a car which was wrecked in a storm in the Pacific two weeks ago. Giant waves crashed on the decks causing much damage to deck cargo.

BIG SEAS MANGLE CARS CARRIED

ONE OF THE smashed cars on the deck of the Amstelveen.

What a waste!

This photo would have been taken in the early 1970s when 8 cwt Minor Vans were still being produced in New Zealand.

shipments in port, or we had to rob engines out of one pack to marry up a particular engine number with a particular chassis number only because the numbers of the vehicle had to match the import licence. As a result of that mix 'n match confusion we had one potentially nasty accident in my domain. The un-packers had taken something out of a crate and assembled it again using only about four nails which the fork hoist driver didn't realise and stacked another case on top of it. As gravity took over, the crate folded immediately and the jolly thing collapsed under the weight opening up like a flower petal, but fortunately no significant damage occurred to the contents. I got the wrap for that one!

"For the amount of stuff we moved over the years we did not damage much at all, most of it happened on the colliers when they got into a storm or heavy seas on car delivery to South Island. From the mid 70's, long after the Minor Van had finished, we assembled Honda Civics

for the NZMC and Daihatsu vehicles under contract, when a ship called *Durham* [or similar] came out from Japan, she struck heavy seas...the mess was incredible, the insurance company had to write the whole C.K.D shipment off. Such accidents did happen occasionally with the British stuff, but as far as I remember it was not too bad at all."

Sometimes they had local supply problems, often also caused by industrial action at the wharf or again by the consequences of import restrictions. If they then ran out of certain stocks, upholstery material for example, they could not finish the batch and had to pull the cars off the line into storage alongside. This was quite a disruption to production, but all that was a lot of "fun" and became a regular part of life in the Assembly Division.

The problem that gave them the biggest headache in the unpacking section were the fixings—nuts, bolts, washers, screws—they

Changing times: Mitsubishi and N.Z.M.C/DOMTRAC *representatives meet in March 1978. Second from left, Mr G. Fraser, centre Sir Walter Norwood, right Mr Sali.*

never arrived in any departmental order and had to be sorted. A section of the store broke it all down using charts and lists attempting to get things in the required order, but after a while it drove them mildly crazy trying to work out the figures. Many years later Eric introduced a simple colour code system that worked much better. Then fasteners were labelled in red — chassis line, green — trim line and so on. "The body shop usually got their lot first, bolts for the doors, guards and so on. Then we delivered to the paint shop those fasteners and small bits that were to be painted prior to assembly. Nearly all other items went to the chassis and trim lines.

At the beginning, before they had any system in place, they tried putting the cartons and bags "on the line", and let the assembly workers help themselves, but ... no that didn't work very well! "A lot of stuff used to go home and that's another story."

The end of Panmure assembly

From the mid-1970s an ever-increasing number of Japanese-designed cars started entering New Zealand as customers demanded something different, rather than the more traditional British designs. Until 1984 around 90,000 locally assembled Japanese cars were sold every year in New Zealand, but by 1987 that figure had

fallen to 70,000, because of increased imports of built-up and second-hand cars from Japan as well as Korea, Italy and Germany. Another important factor at the time was the strength of the Japanese yen, which caused a drop in market share from 85 to 70 per cent.

The Honda Motor Company had over the years slowly increased its shareholding in the NZMC, purchased and later upgraded the former BLMC Assembly Plant in Nelson, and finally gained total control over the organisation. Sadly for the 250 staff at Panmure it was not in Honda's plan to keep the by now aging plant operational. On 30 April 1987 management of the NZMC Limited had to make the announcement that all vehicle production would be relocated to the Nelson plant in order to centralise activities into one plant and to reduce cost. Doors were closed after 34 years of production in April 1988.

Over the years the plant produced the following BMC cars and commercials: the Morris Minor ¼ ton (later 6/8 cwt) van and pick up, a last batch of 27 Morris Minor 1000, the Morris J2 and J4 van or well side, the Morris–Commercial Series III normal & forward control cab/chassis, the Morris-Commercial LC5 cab/chassis, the Morris-Commercial LD 1.5 ton (factory body), the Morris FG/ K30, K40, K60, K80, K100 cab/chassis, the BMC FF and FH 7 or 8 ton, the Wolseley 6/110, the Mini, the Riley Elf and 4/72.

CHAPTER TEN
Neville Brennan: from Office Boy to Plant Manager

eville started in the office at the Newmarket Assembly Division in 1949 as a general office boy. Like everyone else he was on low pay, something like five shillings an hour, roughly ten pound a week. Things didn't improve much in later years either. "Yes, plenty of work and responsibility... it was a very high moral sort of a place, but not high in pay." The years prior to his association with Dominion Motors he worked for Forest Products, did lots of overtime and made good money, which he saved—most of it anyway. This prepared him financially for the years to come. Soon after the factory had started making these then new Morris Minors, I had the desire to own one. If you wanted to buy a new car, you faced a peculiar problem of the times—the No Remittance licence. You could not just walk into a dealership and buy one; no, this only involved people with foreign exchange being granted a licence to import a car. The waiting lists for new vehicles were quite long.

The necessary foreign exchange was in many cases acquired quite legitimately through inheritance, overseas investments and share sales. There were also many dubious schemes, but the authorities of the day didn't appear to be overly concerned how the foreign exchange was acquired.

In those days, if the average person went into a retail outlet and asked to buy a motor-car they would probably just be turned away or put on a long waiting list." I remember visiting my brother-in-law at Schofields [GM agency in the 1950s], I actually witnessed the sales manager coming out of the office followed by a customer and heard him saying in front of many onlookers 'here everyone, he wants to buy a car and has no

[exchange] funds!' He ridiculed the guy because he *wanted to buy*!

"If someone in his position did that today, they'd leg rope him! But not then, it was the aftermath of the war, times were difficult and Government's monetary policies over the years had caused a severe shortage of new cars.

"Despite these difficulties I was fortunate enough to be able to buy a new Minor in '51, a Low-Lite of course, which originally had a price tag of £545. Kindly Dominion Motors gave me a staff discount, so I got it for £515!"

He was very lucky, not many employees were allowed to buy a car, you had to belong to the favoured group, or you had to go through the normal retail channels. In any case staff who bought a car under privilege were not going to sell it on the black market.

"Singles like me could probably save up enough to be able to pay for a new car, but for family men it was generally a lot more difficult, if not impossible.

"The Morris Minor enjoyed a good reputation among the workers, it was easy to assemble, easy to maintain, no great problems and, in its own way, it had character. To my knowledge, we never had a re-call with the Minor, no common or re-occurring problems at all, just the usual little things depending on how fussy the buyer was. The Minor definitely was the preferred model in those days. Yes the occasional one preferred the Oxford, but nine out of ten choose the Minor."

The lucky few could collect a car more or less direct from the factory, after they had cleared all money matters with the Sales Department who had to give it their own road test and register it, but the staff member always knew which car on the line was going to be his, and often it received special treatment from every section during assembly. "Not that we were careless with others, no, just that little bit extra T. L. C."

Dominion Motors was still a small company in the late 1940s which only required a very simple management structure. Richard Andrews, or Dick as staff were allowed to call him, was the boss and in charge of the day to day running of the Assembly Division. He decided on every issue concerning the business, signed every letter that went out, and even decided who could or who could not buy a new car under privilege. He was assisted by three others—Messrs Thompson, Coates, and Finch—who together formed a brilliant team.

Colin Thompson, Technical Supervisor, was a quiet conscientious operator with an incredibly wide range of technical "know how." Neville thinks he started with Andrews when the plant first opened, but if not, he entered very early in the piece.

Maurice Coates 'Morrie', a very "tall yard of pump water", started as a painter and was promoted to Factory Supervisor very quickly. With the Line Foremen reporting to him and being responsible for all staff, his was a busy life. Labour turn over was very high: they had had full employment, a euphemism for labour shortage. "Perhaps he was a bit easy going for the job, but always a gentleman."

T.S. Finch used to be the Company Auditor before joining the Assembly Division. "Conscientious almost to a fault, he ran a very efficient ship, a very efficient pay office including

tight stock control. All accounts were paid on time and the balance sheet was ready for Head Office not later than the weekend after balance date. A marvel of marvels!

"I won't go into details of the Line Foremen, but with not a dud among them it's not too difficult to see why this operation rated in my book as the very tops."

In 1951 Sir Charles Norwood celebrated his 80th birthday and he went right round the whole country visiting all branches. "We were in the office having drinks, when he told us this story of how he had learned things the hard way and how to conduct business."

"He started off reading gas meters in Wellington when he first arrived here from Australia, not a well-paid job, but later he married a few bob which was smart. Then he operated a bad agency for the Willy's vehicles which luckily caught fire and burned to the ground. But his biggest business venture was Dominion Motors, he just opened branches one after another in Auckland, Wellington, Christchurch and Timaru, that was unheard of in the New Zealand motor industry in those days. Then the big Depression hit the world and business was difficult, so the bankers were calling him in a bit. To add to his troubles he had loaned money to his brother-in-law to finance two picture theatres which now also suffered losses and started going down the tubes, so he could not pay Sir Charles. Again, he was telling us that as a lesson. Sir Charles had to foreclose him, he had no option, the banks were breathing down his neck too. His brother in-law said 'OK … it is all yours, if you know how to run a picture theatre better than I do, you can take it!'

"When the bank called Sir Charles in again he told them the same… 'It's all yours, if you can run a motor business better and get something back, it's yours, take it, go on take it!' The bank gave him extended credit!

"He went on to say more about his very busy times as the Mayor of Wellington, and how the stress affected his health. In fact he was verging on a breakdown and his doctor wanted to send him to Australia, told him to go away for a while and relax. Sir Charles said in his own words: 'I knew nobody could run this business like I do,

Mr W.D. (Doug) Gordon

because I've set it all up, but I had no option I had to go away." He appointed W.D. Gordon to look after it while he was on leave. When he returned he found the business had grown, and realised that he had certainly chosen the right man and came to the conclusion that, as long as you are picking the right people for your business, you can't go wrong!"

For quite some period of time Neville hadn't been too happy about some things, mainly the condition in which shipments arrived from the UK, and one day he decided to do something about it, by making some suggestions to The Nuffield Organisation, as it was called then. "Andrews read and signed this particular letter of mine and commented that it was a great suggestion. At that stage I was studying accountancy after work and Dick said to me one day: 'you are in the wrong field fellow, you know, you can handle people!' These words would have some influence on my life some time later.

"Another thing that's typical of Dick is this episode. As I said, I bought my Minor in '51 and then got married in '52. When on the way back from our honeymoon up north, I suggested to my wife to sell the car and use the money for a down-payment on a house. We wanted a family

and decided to go ahead with the plan to sell it, a decision that was not easy to make. When I told my boss T. S. Finch of our intention, he took a deep breath and replied, 'hmmm, you got that car under privilege... I better have a word with Dick first.'

"A few days later I was summoned to Andrew's office... 'Sit down! Mr Finch tells me you are selling your Morris Minor. I can understand why, you bought it under one circumstance as a bachelor, now you are married and come face to face with some responsibility, well...that's your business, you own it, but...if you want another one, *that will be a horse of a different colour*!' End of discussion! We sold the car, bought a house and I was broke for quite some time to come. However, my next vehicle was a second hand Oxford!"

Neville was eventually promoted to Assistant Accountant, but after working in the job for a while he wanted to change from accounting to management, perhaps an idea that was sparked by Dick's earlier words. So he went to night classes at University for a couple nights a week. "Dick Andrews, being Dick Andrews said to me one day, 'well... we pay for your fees and all that sort of thing provided you pass! If you don't...you are history!' I got the message loud and clear, if that was no incentive to put the work in, I don't know what would have been.

"That was Dick Andrews, straight forward, sharp, astute and sometimes tough if need be, but always fair. He controlled the most efficient operation of any in my experience—by far! Always decisive, small in stature, but a big man in attitude and one of Dominion Motors' greatest assets."

Despite having two children, a wife and a mortgage, studies went well and Neville achieved diplomas in Business and Industrial Management—and thanks to Dick Andrews didn't have to raise a loan to get there. "That's why I feel sorry for the current generation, they can't do that, usually they don't get that sort of support from their employer."

Very early after the end of the war Andrews introduced some interesting innovations to DML's staffing policy. Encouraged by Government's rehabilitation scheme for returned servicemen, he employed war amputees who then trained as machinists in the trim shop where they did a great job. Also a couple of blind people were employed in off line sub-assembly work, mostly in the wiring field when production volume was up. Work in these areas had been the prerogative of women, who now worked, and proved adept in all other departments. "The odd sceptical foreman was soon converted. Women now were to be found in the paint shop (rub deck), the mechanical line and the final trim line. From memory it was in the early 50's that women were first employed on the assembly lines on equal pay!

"Not many worked in the body shop, but I can well remember one in particular, who could handle the heavy spot guns as well as any man. Furthermore she was no behemoth, no… in fact she was quite feminine and a marvellous colleague. At a time of acute labour shortage all this proved a real master stroke from Dick Andrews."

Neville soon changed from Accountancy to the Personnel Department and in 1961 became the Factory Manager for the Panmure Assembly Division. When he first got there it was still in the wilderness: horse paddocks, native trees and Mt Wellington in the neighbourhood. "Some Head Office sceptics and people from Management in the Retail Branches referred to this operation as 'Walter's White Elephant', but… Walter Norwood, he sure had the last laugh on that one!"

From inception the Panmure plant operated as a satellite of Newmarket, with an absolute minimum of overheads; management policy, accounting and technical administration were directed from the Newmarket office. It continued very successfully that way up until the formation of the New Zealand Motor Corporation in 1971. Taking their cues also from Andrews, Technical and Accounting provided regular effective service for Panmure, the same high standard as was provided for Newmarket, with no confusion in the lines of communication, responsibility or authority. Andrews in his own inimitable style had his finger on the pulse and kept up with the play by visiting daily. That way he knew exactly the state of health or otherwise of the plant.

"He reported directly to Walter Norwood in Wellington, who of course gave his overall

instructions, but had no part in the daily running of the two plants. Walter Norwood visited frequently and when taken on a factory tour, he showed interest in even minute technical details. He and Andrews got on very well over the years, and together made up the best Management Team there ever was in Dominion Motors. Between them in rank was the General Manager W.D. Gordon, Ex-Accountant, a hard working, hard driving man. Oh…he was a wild 'bugger', he made many people's work lives a bloody misery, but Andrews himself took little notice and by-passed him often, simply overrode his authority. Because of Walter Norwood's and Dick Andrews' association we here in Auckland were pretty well immune to Gordon's influence."

Compared to Newmarket's Assembly Division, Panmure first was a smaller operation, less staff and less output initially. "We produced mainly commercial vehicles in the late 'fifties, many different models at quite low production runs. At the beginning manufacturing methods were often basic, just to make do for the moment. Things were temporary and got changed often

WOMEN LEND A HAND

An average of 35 women are employed at this plant on a wide variety of jobs. They are paid at male workers' rates. Here a motor is hoisted on to a trolley before being fitted to the motor body.

as production of yet another model required. Body panels came from the pack slightly oily and had to be put through a chemical degreasing process before they could be used. This was still done manually using large flat tanks and one poor guy's job it was to wash them down. The other plant already operated a semi-automatic degreasing system, I think it was the first of its kind in our industry, designed and installed by our own factory supervisor, Colin Thompson. But out here things were still a bit under developed in that regard. I can still remember a Scotch fellow—Jack, his name, I had to fire him in the end, but in retrospect I was wrong to do so, in fact we were all wrong, because he was 'high' with the fumes by the afternoon. Working conditions in his area were a bit primitive, no extractor fans—nothing, just a booth. The solvents were strong and quite aggressive, can't say what type it was, that's too long ago. Occasionally I still see Jack here in Auckland, but he will not speak to me—can't blame him, really! I remember his wife coming round to my office saying what a good man and Christian he is, but I told her that he could not go on the way he's

going as he was totally defiant. He was the poor victim of the fact that we had no ventilation, no protection at all. Well... I realised that much later.

"We received our instructions, what model to build, what quantity and colours, from Head Office in Wellington and depending on the state of the Import License at the time, production fluctuated quite a bit according to the balance of trade. Out of the blue the Minister of Customs announced cut-backs in licences and as a result of that we had to reduce production, which also meant a reduction in staff. There was no such thing as severance, or any form of compensation for the individuals affected, that was tough. In those days it was my job to break the news, to walk around the lines and tell them, 'sorry you and you are gone!' At one occasion I had to make a severe cut-back of 25 percent. The decision who to make redundant was always hard and never taken lightly, because we were a close team and enjoyed good relations. We tried to lessen the impact for the person concerned by taking their personal circumstances into account. The balance was often tipped if a person had a partner in a good job elsewhere and was not the only

An average of 35 women were employed at the Newmarket plant on a wide variety of jobs. They were paid at male workers' rates. Opposite is a news clipping showing a motor/gearbox unit being hoisted before fitting to the car. Below is a photo showing mainly women employed as machinists in the so-called trim shop, seen here sewing seat covers.

money earner for the family. The unfortunate ones often could find other jobs easy enough, work was plentiful, but at the same time that particular worker might have been excellent and experienced for many tasks and had their roots and friends here, that made the decision hard for both of us.

"At other times, when the Government was in a more favourable mood we had increased production, we frantically hired staff and quickly trained them on the job, that usually worked best. Regular training seminars for our charge hands ensured their ability to get the key points across to a new staff member. This was an ongoing problem, because we had a terrific staff turnover in those uncertain times.

"The prevailing labour shortage put the workers in a reasonably powerful situation, but despite that, they did not abuse the Unions, at least not at DML. We had a very good relationship with the unions, which were no push-overs, but at the same time not overly aggressive either. The atmosphere was good, we had a great record, something I can't say about the rest of the New Zealand industry. Things changed many years later, when management introduced a bonus incentive scheme, we did have problems with that, negotiating the number of hours allowed for each model and so on. Some near misses happened when Dominion Motors became part of the New Zealand Motor Corporation and we became much more bureaucratic and governored by new-style-know-all management. As the DML we had no major industrial action at all. Our management never suggested cutting corners or tried to compromise working conditions. Dick Andrews would not buy that, but on the other hand it was not a holiday camp either, you had to work hard, the owners wanted their 'pound of flesh' too. We expected a decent day's pay and the boss wanted a decent day's work out of us.

"So the years went by without major changes until in 1971 a merger between several English car makers in New Zealand was announced to form a strong alliance known as the New Zealand Motor Corporation (NZMC). And how the climate at DML changed after that!

"Management from the 'Ivory Tower' became the order of the day; obsession with power and control led to a top-heavy management structure, quite remote from the base operation. It quickly became a case of 'Head Office knows best' and daily reports from Auckland to Wellington were instituted. Then followed reviews, more reviews, assessments, more assessments and one hell of a lot of 'navel gazing'.

"One guy, ex Austin became the big chief of it all, a nice bloke personally, but a 'bean counter' through and through. He had a great big chart in his office with pins in all colours in the rainbow. We used to be called down to their Head Office for meeting after meeting, wasting time, playing the game. They requested daily reports on the state of affairs. The last hour of every day I had to send three guys round the factory, take stock here and there, everywhere in the plant. They had to have data on the C.K.D stocks in store, where the boxes were and where in the factory unpacked stocks were. They wanted a count of produced cars...oh!

"One fellow had to drive out to get the last flight to Wellington—*every day*! It was costing us a fortune, but no, they had to have their pins moved daily. That never stopped and was more important than producing good cars. As we now know it stopped eventually!

"Coming from a situation where Dick Andrews reported to Walter Norwood it was simple a clean-cut deal, but this was utterly frustrating to say the least. The inevitable result was that the small grievances, being unattended and ignored, became major issues. The industrial rot set in—and in a big way! Luckily by that time I had long since been divorced from the debacle."

Neville Brennan with Sir Walter Norwood shows Peter Shore, British Under-Secretary for Trade, around the Newmarket assembly plant.

CHAPTER ELEVEN

Bruce S. Carson: from Car Salesman to Chief Executive

ruce Carson's father was a barrister and solicitor in Dunedin where Bruce grew up as a child. His father had his own practice and Bruce's initial intention was to follow him into law.

In 1953 Bruce's father was appointed a stipendiary magistrate in Wellington and in 1954 Bruce joined his mother and father after two years at Otago University. The incentive to work with his father passed with this appointment and having always been passionate about cars he decided on a change in direction. He suggested to his father he would like to follow a career in the motor industry.

Even though Bruce applied for positions with General Motors and the Ford Motor Company, his father arranged for him to meet Arthur Lee, the Dominion Motors Company Secretary, who he had met socially. "This resulted in me joining the company as a second hand car salesman starting at the Kent Terrace showroom on 10 January 1955. At the same time I enrolled as a part time B.Com student at Victoria University."

After 18 months on sales, as part of a training programme Bruce was moved to the workshop office as a claims clerk and then to the administration office in Courtenay Place.

In 1958 some of the senior sales staff at the branch left rather suddenly and he was "thrown in the deep end" as the used car sales manager, again at Kent Terrace. "We had a good, enthusiastic team who were all prepared to not only sell cars, but to also groom them, repair punctures and change tyres, even carry out valve grinds at the back of the showroom, while all the time having a lot of fun."

They had been well taught in the art of selling cars. "During my first 18 months as a salesman I

remember standing behind one of the pillars in the showroom listening to the senior salesman, Peter Stratford, conclude sales. He was most effective and I learnt much from his methods. We would normally ask a customer if they knew the type of car they were looking for: was it for a family use or a personal runabout, did they have a price in mind and so on. We then tried to find a car that would match up with their requirements and always assumed that they wanted to buy, so we were always positive. The price of our car was always the last thing mentioned. We really worked hard at trying to make ourselves friends of our customers so that we obtained repeat business and referrals. Our training also emphasised product knowledge, being able to point out all the positive features and an ability to answer all the customer's questions."

The new car business was a completely different scene with long waiting lists and the trade in general had a reputation of shady dealings. "The public had to wait donkey's years to buy a new car unless they had overseas funds or a good trade. Customers would come into the showroom to enquire how they were progressing on the waiting list, only to be told to come back in 12 months — dreadful!"

However, back to used cars in the late 1950s. "Most of our cars sold for £100-300, nothing very expensive and not large profit margins but because of volume the Company made a good return." Every six months they did a complete stock check where detail and accuracy were insisted upon. Cost, price, reconditioning and other direct expenses had to be clearly tabulated for the General Manager, Company Secretary, Branch Manager and Marketing Manager so that they could appraise each car for stock purposes. "It was a most amusing sight seeing this group 'in line of stern' walking around the used car lot pricing the stock to reflect the management's financial intentions for the year's results. As 'tail end Charlie' I had to ensure everything was correct and in order. Such was the control and discipline."

When Bruce joined the Company it had a constant stream of second hand Morris Series E models and low-light Minors traded in. Then later the 1951 high headlight model with two-piece windscreen and side valve engine. "The side valve was a great engine, reliable but without a great deal of performance. The first 803cc overhead valve engines had more get up and go, but tended to be driven harder at higher revs. These 'oil droppers' as they were known, resulted in plenty of warranty claims on engines and gearboxes."

The Morris Minor 1000 of 1957 with its 948cc engine, bigger windscreen and other features was a vast improvement. "It still kept the service department busy and, yes, there were oil leaks and left rear hub oil seal claims, but we never thought of it other than being a wonderful car. We believed the flamboyant advertising slogans to be true and that our company had the best products."

Dominion Motors generally sold cars to the private purchaser — the "little old lady with the blue hair rinse" as the saying goes. "Private people tended to drive their cars more carefully so they lasted longer and that is why our products and the Company had such a good name. I can honestly say we saw the Morris Minor as being a car that could justifiably be regarded as good as, if not better than any other in its class — well finished for a car of its time and not likely to cause after sales problems. By the way my first car which I purchased from the Company was a 1938 Morris 8 in which I never exceeded 35 mph! Next was a '52 side valve Minor which I converted to a 948cc engine for hill climbs and beach races."

Because Dominion Motors was an importer, assembler, distributor and retailer, it was a company with many cost and profit centres. Known more as a private company it was well thought of by the public with Sir Charles and Sir Walter highly regarded and recognized. "As employees we were well treated and respected and many of the industry's top people over the years can lay claim to spending some of their formative years working for Dominion Motors. When Mr Lee employed me he said to a raw 20-year-old, 'Some day, Mr Carson, you will have your own dealership!' I replied 'I would like to stay all my life with this company, Mr Lee.' I did."

Dominion Motors was not known for ever making excessive profits, but in its diversified activities it was a financially successful company, especially with the government licensing regime. "The assembly plants were expected to show a small surplus and with distributor and retail margins combined, a mark up of 30–35% was normal. A new car customer was expected to trade-in their old car, but I never felt we took advantage of those customers in the price we paid for the trade. On a used Morris Minor we might have made £80–100 on a car selling for £550. With new cars so keenly sought after, second hand models sometimes sold for more than the new price. A customer with no-remittance funds was therefore always a winner. We often paid them more for their trade-in than what they paid for the new car."

By 1962 Bruce had become Wellington Branch

MORRIS MINOR
Facts for Salesmen

Your "walk around" sales guide. Starting from the left-hand-side front door handle, we walk round the car in a clockwise direction, pointing out the features as we go.

Sales Manager for both new and second-hand cars and for the next 6–7 years was part of a successful sales team. On occasion it exceeded 100 used units per month from the Kent Terrace used car outlets, and record new car sales.

In 1969 he became acting General Manager of Dominion Motors nationally at the time when the merger arrangements forming The New Zealand Motor Corporation were being finalised.

The Corporation was formed through the merging of the five Austin and Morris distributing companies in New Zealand. Seabrook Fowlds Ltd, (Auckland region), Magnus Motors Ltd (Wellington region), David Crozier Ltd (Canterbury and Otago regions), P.H.Vickery Ltd (Southland region), were Austin Distributors and Dominion Motors Ltd, nationally, was the Morris distributor. Each merging company had distributor-owned retail branches in various centres, as well as a network of independent franchised dealers. The Austin companies had a shareholding in Austin Distributors Federation Ltd, the company that operated their common vehicle assembly plant in Petone, Wellington. Some of these companies also brought other franchises to the merger eg, Rambler in Wellington. Dominion Motors as the national Morris importer was the strongest of the merging companies with a series of large retail branches.

In 1952 Morris and Austin had amalgamated in the United Kingdom as BMC and in the late 1960s the New Zealand companies were urged by BMC to merge similarly. "It was probably the right thing to do in any case as the era of licensing was generally drawing to a close and the world was starting to see the effect the Japanese auto industry was bringing to competition." BMC brought Leyland heavy trucks under its umbrella as BLMC and their New Zealand operations including the Nelson plant which assembled Leyland, Rover, Triumph, Land Rover and Jaguar were bought by the Corporation in 1972. Following this the Corporation's franchises accounted for around one third of the country's new car sales.

During the first three years of the Corporation's existence the country was divided into three fairly autonomous regions with branches and dealers in those areas under the control of regional managers who were responsible for sales, performance, vehicle allocations and finance. Johnny Seabrook, previously Managing Director of Seabrook Fowlds Ltd, headed the northern region; George Thiele, the Managing Director of David Crozier Ltd in the south, and Bruce the central area. The regions had their own parts and service managers as well as accounting, information systems, and personnel services.

It was felt by some in the Head Office that the Corporation would be better served in the future if the structure of the company did not rely so much on the regions which were seen to be too powerful. The consulting firm McKinsey & Co. were contracted to prepare a report and as a result of this, in 1973 the company structure was divisionalised in Assembly and Supply, Marketing, Administration, Personnel, Retail and remained in this form until the early 1980s.

By 1976 the dominance of the Japanese Auto Industry in world markets resulted in the Corporation adding Honda cars to its list of British franchises. As Honda Sales Manager Bruce was responsible for setting up the dealer network, liaising with the Assembly Division on specifications and volume, supply of parts and service provision. "This was a fascinating job marketing a fabulous franchise. Then in the later stages of the decade I was appointed the Retail Divisional Manager and subsequently the Marketing Manager."

In the early 1950s advertisements like these appeared nearly every second day in New Zealand's major newspapers throughout the country. These are dated May and June 1951.

In July 1953 the Morris Minor was still advertised together with the Oxford (above) but from then on the models were promoted on their own. The Morris Six was no longer advertised in the daily papers.

These ads were published in 1957 (above) and 1961 (right).

By this stage the corporation had started to purchase companies that were not directly involved in motor activities, such as Healings (bicycles) and Group Rentals (TV and video). It had also divisionalised its heavy truck business under the name DOMTRAC which had much earlier represented Dominion Motors' interest in trucks, earthmoving equipment and a myriad of other lines. DOMTRAC was a shortening of "Dominion Motors Industrial & Tractor Equipment Company Limited" which Bruce knew well as a newly appointed employee— "we had to physically count all the spare pars every six months and then extend and calculate the values."

Because of the acquisition of non-motor businesses it was decided to change the name of the Company from "New Zealand Motor Corporation Ltd" to "EMCO Group Ltd". This was a clever way to label the organization while still sounding like the previous name. As an abbreviation the Corporation had often been

referred to as NZMC, so when EMCO was formed in 1982, the Motor Division, which still represented over 60% of the business, became a separate subsidiary company as NZMC Limited. Bruce was appointed the General Manager and later Chief Executive. As a publicly listed company EMCO had substantial assets in land and buildings as well as many profitable trading operations. As such it was attractive to a possible purchaser as the shareholding was predominantly held by institutions and individuals. After an attempt by one organization, the shareholding in EMCO was purchased by Steel & Tube Holdings Ltd in 1985. STH subsequently sold off some of the subsidiary companies and divisions, but initially retained NZMC. Honda took a 25% interest in NZMC but by 1988 most of the Japanese franchises were controlled by the parent companies in Japan and the Honda Motor Company bought all NZMC's Honda interests, including some of the retail branches, the Nelson assembly plant, vehicle and

A fleet of 10 new Morris 8 cwt vans is purchased by Taylor's Dry Cleaners of Wellington. Ten Morris 8 cwt vans with mileages ranging from 20,000 to 100,000 were traded in. The Managing Director of Taylor Brothers Ltd, John Taylor, said he was pleased with the performances of the vans in a 20,000 mile a year stop-start city service. The new fleet was supplied by Wellington Morris Sales and Service, Courtenay Place. The photo shows the central region manager, Bruce Carson (left) shaking hands with the Managing Director of Taylor Brothers Ltd, Mr J. Taylor and handing over the key for one of the vans in the new fleet. Looking on is Mr A. Ross, Morris Sales Branch Manager.

parts stock. It also offered positions to many of the staff.

This left NZMC holding just its Rover and Land Rover franchises. Although sales volumes were reasonable for a European franchise and the organization was controlled by just a few dedicated anglophiles, the Company still had substantial assets in buildings and land which had not been sold when Honda bought the Honda interests. Steel & Tube therefore decided to move out of the motor business and did this by closing NZMC, selling the properties, and quitting stock by entering into a joint venture operation with Colin Giltrap and John Fairhall, known as Motorcorp Holdings Ltd which, with other franchises, maintained a distribution set up in Auckland for Rover and Land Rover.

Steel & Tube subsequently sold their interests to the other partners while BMW bought and then sold Rover in the United Kingdom. New Rover cars are no longer imported into New Zealand. Land Rover is owned by Ford; Honda have closed their assembly operations at Nelson and achieve a much reduced market share than in the NZMC days, and Austin and Morris brands have long since passed.

Bruce coments: "The closure of NZMC spelt the end of a long family heritage since the early days of motoring in New Zealand, and because it suited me, it also spelt the end of my 36 years in the trade. I retired from it all in 1991, perhaps a little sad, but that is life!"

Left: The DOMTRAC plant in Panmure with a range of its products on display.
Below: The Nelson-based assembly division of British Leyland, later Honda.

CHAPTER TWELVE

John McKillop: from Public Servant to Office Manager

Dominion Motors used to dispatch many of their Morris vehicles from Tamaki railway station in Auckland where John McKillop worked from 1956 onwards. The dispatch clerks from DML were almost daily customers, always looking to make bookings for rolling stock. John knew one of them, Rod, quite well, because he and John had been at school together. "We often had a bit of a chat about things and work, that's how I got to know a bit about his employer. Somehow he made life in the private sector seem more interesting than life in the Public Service, in my case the Railways."

It was through the regular contact at the station that John became more and more interested in Dominion Motors. "In 1961, I guess, he may have mentioned that they were looking for an office clerk, but anyway, after five years with the NZR, and realising that I would never become an engine driver, I left them, because DML gave me the opening I wanted." Ron Stone, the ex-Plant Supervisor had taken over from Dick Andrews, who retired, and was now the Assembly Division's Manager. He was seeking to employ an accounting student: no problem, John quickly enrolled as such and started studying accountancy by correspondence—not a good move! Doing study this way meant that you had to set your own timetable and, unless you are quite strong in this area, the temptation to leave study and assignments until tomorrow was only too easy. John got the job.

His work place at DML in Panmure was the Front Office where he busied myself as a costing clerk. They had some, by today's standards, ancient Burroughs adding machines and a Friden calculator, which performed multiplication and subtraction functions mechanically. Kids with

computers today would be amazed.

There were about 90 people on staff at that time and every one knew everyone else. "DML was a really friendly place to work. Active Social Clubs were at both Newmarket and Panmure Plants. At each, indoor bowls was played during the lunch hour. The tournaments always had a great following, even those not playing would keep an eye on the competition. A walk to the body shop at the far end of the plant would take an age by the time you had discussed the problems of the world with those you passed on the way there and back. We were not too rushed, something I was quite used to from the Railways."

The costing function required that all labour and materials were recorded against the production lot they were used in. At the end of the run a comparison was made between actual

Above: A Minor van reaches the end of assembly.
Right: The DML Cricket Club of 1951-52.

usage and the bill of material. This was often a problem! In one case, at the Newmarket plant, the cost clerk was going over the costing of a lot with Sef, Thomas Sefton Finch, the Accountant. He was a real gentleman—an accountant from the old school—he used to come out to Panmure specially to count the petty cash and, with this lot, he was telling the clerk, that he noticed there were no tyres booked against it. The clerk, "a bit of a lad", looked Sef straight in the eye and said, "Oh, that was the Minor batch they sent out on bare rims". Sef looked at him and said, "They *wouldn't* do that *would* they?" In the end, he got to the bottom of the mystery and the lot was charged with the tyres that had been used, John thinks.

There was one occasion at Panmure when a quarter-ton Minor van reached the end of the assembly line and was due to be started up for its very first time. Several attempts to fire it up failed, the starter motor just could not crank the engine over. "On investigation it was discovered that the sump was devoid of oil, but on the other hand one or more cylinders were full of it. The assembler who had the task of putting the oil in had a little trouble that day distinguishing the oil filler hole from the spark plug holes through an alcohol induced haze. He did not work for the company much longer."

Ron Stone's full name was Ronald Joseph Stone, but he was frequently referred to as "Ronald Joseph". Not within his hearing if possible. He had regular times when he went in to Newmarket Assembly Division, and one day, when he was supposedly there, John walked in to the office and did not notice that he had returned early and was standing in the far corner. "I asked Marlene, the Receptionist, 'Is Ronald Joseph back yet?' A voice boomed out from behind me, 'Yes, I *am*!' There was a red face on my part, and grins all round the office."

The Minor and the Oxford saloons were produced at the Newmarket plant and the quarter ton (later called the 6 cwt) van and pick up models were assembled at Panmure. The vehicles were given a test drive around the local streets for a couple of miles to ensure that everything appeared OK. Once the vehicles were cleared by the Chief Inspector they were ready for delivery. Those going to the Auckland Branch in Broadway (retail outlet) would be collected by a team from there. Those going to places in the rest of North Island would be sent by rail. For South Island deliveries shipping was used, usually in the form of colliers returning from Onehunga (South Auckland) to Westport or Greymouth. Before shipping a wax coating was applied to the cars to protect against salt spray. Once the vehicles arrived they would be railed or sometimes convoy driven to the nearest town. In later years, from about '63 onwards, Car Haulaways started up in business with their road transporters and they took deliveries directly from the plants. The first transporter to take vehicles from Panmure had a load of nine Minis on board.

All vehicles we made were pre-ordered (remember it was very difficult to get a vehicle in those days) and the delivery address of each unit produced was known before the lot was put into production. They had a range of body trim/paint colour options and the retail side of

The Panmure Assembly Division's office building as seen in 1957. Working conditions inside were very basic then.

Dominion Motor's business told them what ratios they required for each option from each run. They would then plan the run accordingly. At Panmure, they were, at one time, doing separate runs for each model being built so they might have a lot of OT vans, another of J2s, and some 7 ton trucks being built at the same time. It was a challenge to see if the forward planning could get the vehicles to be painted the same colour to the paint shop at the same time in order to reduce the need for paint changes. This was of course in the days before there were computers to help with scheduling.

"Production runs were frequently set at around 240 units per lot — but this was really only for costing purposes, particularly at Newmarket. There, there were two lines, one doing Oxfords and the other Minors and basically, there was no break between the production runs. From memory I would estimate the Morris Minor production at anything up to 30 vehicles per day (I'm really not sure about that), but I do know that each assembler in Newmarket had about a 15-minute job cycle."

At Panmure the daily production was considerably fewer than at Newmarket and, with various models coming down the line alternately the job cycle was somewhat longer — perhaps an hour or so. It was found that staff members who worked well in one plant sometimes had difficulty coping with the different work flow in the other.

The car assembly business was very much carried out at the whim of the politicians of the day. "There would be tightening of credit, imports would be squeezed and we would be worried about having to put staff off. Then there would be an abrupt turn around and we would be frantically hiring new staff and working overtime to meet targets, or to make the most of the imports that had suddenly been made available under the Import Licensing Scheme. Our staff turnover was terrific, which called for constant training programmes. We had a

Above: John McKillop's view from the office window. A small shipment is leaving by train which consists of three Morris FG K30, one Minor van, one Wolseley 6/99 and a Nuffield tractor.
Below: The first car transporter is being inspected by those who had nothing better to do at the time. At the far right is a young Neville Brennan and right in the white labcoat is Cyril Atherton, Chief Inspector.

supervisors' staff training session one time at Panmure, which was conducted by the Plant Manager Neville Brennan and Claude P. [name withheld]. In fact, we, the attendees, thought it was being run solely by Neville. The course concerned supervision and staff relations. At one stage of the proceedings Claude burst in to the session and started talking to Nev. Soon, a heated argument developed between them resulting in (a) Claude being told off and (b) everyone in the room feeling really quite embarrassed. This, it turned out, was what was supposed to happen—

Nev. and Claude were putting on a really good act to graphically demonstrate why you should air your differences in private and not bawl out another staff member in public. It worked really well.

"It was most fascinating hearing Claude, a couple of days later and from a reasonable distance, bawling out the plant's caretaker in a hallway for omitting to do something."

In 1966 John left the Company to get more accounting experience, this time at University. After he had finally passed all his exams he went

The assembly of Morris J4 and Morris Minor vans at Panmure. The front van has just had its road wheels fitted and has rolled off the assembly line.

to visit Ron Stone to get a certificate of service signed. "He passed me a piece of paper and said that, while he was doing what I asked of him, I should read the paper. It was an advert looking for someone to replace Sef Finch the Accountant, who had retired. After I had a read, Ron said, 'Now go and apply for it!'"

John did exactly that and one day, not expecting it, received a late call at home. Being in a silly mood at the time he answered the phone with "Howick Looney Bin", or similar.

"The caller was Mr A.B. Smith, the Secretary in Head Office, inviting me to come down to Wellington for a job interview. I thought aaah..., well so much for that; anyway I went down by plane, a Viscount, the first time I'd ever flown in one of those. I recall large big windows and sitting more or less on the wing in line with the blades. I thought, well...if one of those things flicks off...! In Wellington I got the job and began another bout with DML, or NZMC as it had become, in 1970, this time as Office Manager (they had dropped the 'Accountant' title) based in Newmarket. Some time later I left the Assembly Division and transferred to the British Leyland operation in Mt Wellington. It was from there that I became one of an increasing number who left the organisation in 1974. It was no longer the Company we had come to know!"

The variety of vehicles produced at Panmure required very skilled assembly workers able to switch from one job to another.

CHAPTER THIRTEEN
John Lytollis: from Assembly Worker to Paint Inspector

During the last year of World War II John Lytollis was based in Egypt. He came home to New Zealand in 1946 and worked as a postman for a couple of years, until he found a more lucrative job installing thermal insulation. "We were using asbestos in those days, not knowing about the health risks involved with the stuff, so we worked without protection for our lungs, a mistake that did cost me my health in intervening years," he says.

In 1954 Dominion Motors was taking on staff for their new Panmure Assembly Plant, just at the right time for John, because he had enough of the insulation job. He decided to change jobs, worked for DM the next four years and then again for one year in the mid-sixties. "Workers were in demand in those days and changing jobs was not a worry, like it is today."

The first task John was trained for was the installation of the wiring looms and other electrical components into the brand new Morris Minor vans. "You had to climb all over that thing, crawl underneath and inside the cab to get the best advantage points to reach the remotest places behind the dash-panel. Kneeling on the floor pan for a long time was a pain, but otherwise the job was not too hard," he recalls. After a few months working in this section he got bored "fiddling" with wires and showed more interest in the mechanical side of the assembly process. His supervisors recognised this and began training him in nearly all other sections of the plant with two exceptions, the Trim- and Paint-Shops. Somehow he always preferred to do the mechanical assembly work, and his favourite job became the installation of the column gear change on the Morris J2 Vans, in which he specialised. After he was taught the

skill of operating the heavy spot guns and the art of gas welding, he helped out in the Body-Shop, doing such things as fusing the door pillars to the roof and the hinge posts to the flitch panel. There were two or three guys on one jig (most of the time) doing a physically demanding job—probably the hardest work of all sections—but John enjoyed his time there.

The panels were unpacked from the crates and put through a degreasing process before they were brought to them clean and ready to use. This was done in large tanks filled with trichloroethylene, a horrible smelling solvent. Elements at the bottom of the tank heated the chemical to up to about 40 degrees Celcuis to increase its effectiveness, and the vapour that rose from it was condensed back into liquid by

In this section of the body shop the bodies were mounted onto the chassis.

cooling elements around the top rim of the tank, designed to stop the stuff from escaping. It nearly worked, but not one hundred percent, as a result it slowly filled the air with its horrible dry-cleaner-like smell.

The edges of each panel had to be ground clean from primer for the spot-welds to take properly. For each different car model they produced there, they had construction jigs to hold body panels in place for welding. In the case of the Minor Van, which John worked on most of the time, they had one jig set up for the cab and another for the back end, the van- or wellside body. Their jigs were strong and reasonably accurate steel constructions "homemade" from right-angled or T-shaped sections. The whole thing was often bolted to the concrete floor for added strength and safety. This formed the so-called jig base, a reliable and perfectly level foundation for the assembly of motor-car bodies free from distortion and twist. Attached to this base frame were a number of mounts to cradle the floor pans, and also brackets, some fixed permanently, others removable to allow the body to come out of the "mould". These brackets gave them reliable

points of reference as to where exactly the panels should go, without measuring every time, and they assured the correct positioning and clamping of all body panels for welding. They also used smaller, portable brackets, particularly inside a cab or body, mainly for cross bracing. Some panels, for example the "B" post, had a small hole pressed into the bottom flange, which had to line up with another hole in the outer of the two under-sill halves. A prodder (pointed pin) was then pushed through both holes and moved around until the panels lined up correctly. Before welding the post to the roof, the accurate shape of the door opening was established, again, with the help of a jig-frame. Other panels were often guided into place by their own particular shape; the roof skin or the dashboard panel are good examples. All body panels remained in the jig until fully assembled, welded and even the doors fitted and adjusted for correct clearance to the guards.

They didn't have to build the cars completely from scratch; in the case of the Minor Van the chassis frames and also the cab floor pans came out of the box pre-assembled and primed by

Nuffield Metal Works. They were complete with sills, boxing plates, lower cab rear section, everything upwards as far as the toe board cross member, ready to mount onto the jig base and ready to accept the rest of the body work, at least so was the plan. Sometimes panels didn't fit and required extra attention, a little trim with the snips or panel beating after they had suffered a hard time on the boat from England, but this was the exception rather than the rule. Really badly damaged pressings were sorted out already in the unpacking area and probably written off. The most likely panels to suffer transport damage were the front guards, but steel was thick then and things could be repaired. "I remember, a few years later, the Minis, when you ran your fingers along the inside of the roof skin, you could 'see' them on the outside, so thin were the pressings then."

After his time in the Body-Shop the Division's Manager, Ron Stone, promoted John to the position of Leading Hand and gave him the responsibility for the Minor ¼-ton mechanical assembly. "I was in charge of a little less than a dozen workers, a number that fluctuated a lot according to workload, and that depended

ultimately on Government policy and the status of the No-Remittance Licences. Our output was never constant because of the licences, but on average, and given the circumstances, it seems that we produced a lot of vehicles, for commercial use or the lucky private owner with money available from overseas. In most cases the average Kiwi Bloke couldn't buy new anyway, he had to go for a second hand car, if he could afford one at all."

In John's section they fitted the body onto the chassis and later the running gear into it all. Some of them would work on the line, others would do the pre-assembly of under-car things like the fitting of leave springs to the diff, tyres to the rims, front suspension and torsion bars. Most of the bolts fixing the cab to the chassis were easy to install, but the ones at the very front had to go through three panels—the chassis, the tie plate and the engine mount; that often required a bit of brute force, again with the trusty prodder, until the bolts went through. "Another trouble spot were the tapped holes for the front shock absorbers, the threads were usually clogged with thick primer, applied to prevent things from rusting during shipping, but for us a real

Not Panmure, but Newmarket Minor 1000 assembly. This picture demonstrates clear the consruction of a jig base which was similar for the cab/chassis version.

BEST small van buy!

...and no other light van makes a gallon of petrol *do so much work*

70 cubic feet of easily-accessible space . . . Independent Front-Wheel Suspension . . . Telescopic Rear Shock Absorbers and dozens of other features make these Morris Vans an outstanding business proposition.

SEE THE
MORRIS ¼ ton
VAN & PICK-UP

N.Z. Distributors: **THE DOMINION MOTORS LTD.**
Head Office, Courtenay Place, Wellington and at Auckland, Christchurch and Timaru
DEALERS EVERYWHERE
Representing: NUFFIELD EXPORTS LTD. (Chairman: Sir Leonard Lord)

all running gear was fitted we had to bleed the brake system, as well as temporarily set the toe-in for the steering. In case of the first, a container with brake fluid was screwed onto the reservoir of the master cylinder, which was then hooked up to a small hand pump used to pressurise the container and fill the brake system. This operation was always a mystery, we knew how many strokes on the pump it would take, and most cars were OK after that, but sometimes we had to do it again and again 'till it felt right. If anything was wrong, Chief Inspector, Cyril Atherton, at the end of the production line rejected it and the car came back with a note on the wind-screen."

For the second task, the initial alignment of the steering, they used a tight string, from the rear drums past the front ones, centred the rack, and adjusted the steering rod ends until the drums lined up parallel to the string. John always gave it half a turn extra each side of the rod-end trying to get toe-in spot on.

"Cyril's team, of course, had the proper gear to check and re-adjust them before the vehicle left the factory. He often told me later how close to the exact setting my adjustments were. I took great pride in that.

"If I remember correctly, we probably did 10 to 15 Minor Vans or Pick-ups in one day, if we did Minors only, but normally we had quite a mix of models on the line, therefore production numbers for this model alone are sketchy."

The team's overall performance relied heavily on everyone's skill and motivation. To encourage higher production Dominion Motors introduced a bonus system, based on the number of cars produced. If they had met the target for the day, all staff involved received an additional payment, perhaps an extra ten shillings each, perhaps about $20 in today's money. The experienced workers could easily swap from one model to another. In Newmarket they did Minors or Oxfords in bigger lots, all day long the same thing, but they did smaller lots in Panmure and had to be very flexible. "Most workers had their favourite jobs, something they were particularly good at, we made sure that they remained in that area. Some of the guys could fit and adjust a bonnet in only a few seconds, the skill usually doesn't impress outsiders, but if you

nuisance. Anyway, they had to be re-tapped before we could get the bolts in, and sometimes, when we were in a rush the assembler got the bit cross threaded, forced it and broke it off, which meant a hold up and lots of extra work." Often the only way to remove the broken piece was to make a larger hole into the toe board cross member from the opposite angle and to punch it out. "In any case it was a hassle when it happened, but in time we learnt from our mistakes and paid more attention to that particular area."

Another stage in the assembly was the fitting of the engine/gearbox units, an easy job that took them only a few minutes per car. "We had it down to a fine art, I would lower the unit into the engine bay, and a mate would guide the drive shaft through the big opening in the cross member. Once in place, a bit of shoving and pushing did the trick and the bolts went in. After

The mechanical assembly takes place in the background while the front vehicle has the headliner fitted.

Below: The Minor Van and the Mini assembled next to each other in the early 1960s.

get the inexperienced bloke on the job, he could do a lot of costly damage and pull the average for the whole team down. Quite often, when the Company employed a new assembler, things could go wrong. He might have been working too close to the windscreen and not realising the danger until suddenly, the tempered glass

'exploded' into bits with a bang! Other times a worker would drill accidentally into the wire loom and later when the battery was connected the whole thing started to smoke. We used to cheer the embarrassed guy and gave them hell, but all in good taste. One day a young chap wanted to shift a van in the yard and crashed it,

Above: The Panmure Assembly Division in 1957—still plenty of room to play sports.
Below: The new vehicle yard.

that way we found out that he could not drive, obviously, but the damaged guard was quickly replaced and everything put back to normal before Ron Stone, the Manager, did his rounds. Nobody leaked a word and he never found out. We were a good team and good mates and it was a good company to work for."

Life there was not only hard work, and they made sure we had moments of fun and relaxation as well. Sport played a major roll during lunch breaks. The Company owned very large paddocks surrounding the plant, reaching to the foot of Mt Wellington, where they used to play football or cricket whenever they could. Many

employees were also active members of the social club organising all sorts of events, such as outings and dances.

After four years "on the line", John left Dominion Motors to seek his fortune elsewhere, but a number of years later he was offered the position of Paint Inspector, which he took and held for one year. By that time the climate in the organisation had changed and working there was not the same anymore.

John asserts, "I'm confident that, given the opportunity again, I could still assemble a Minor Van today!"

CHAPTER FOURTEEN

Ross L. George: from Management Trainee to Branch Manager

fter graduating from Scots College in Wellington, Ross George joined his Grandfather's company, The Dominion Motors Ltd, in 1953 as a Management Trainee. During the following five years he studied Accountancy at Victoria University part time and worked in all facets of the Company, including Head Office, Parts, Workshop and New and Used Car Sales, eventually becoming the Used Car Sales Manager at the Wellington Branch.

Soon after his hands-on training he embarked on an 18-month "overseas experience" to further his knowledge in the motor industry. Ross was lucky The Dominion Motors held the Pontiac franchise which while only a small portion of the business, nevertheless gave him access to General Motors and he was able to spend three months at Vauxhall, Luton (England) on a Dealer Management course. On completion of that he went to Nuffield Exports in Oxford for a further three months of work experience which involved processing the orders from international Morris Distributors. This was complicated by the fact that very few countries had the same specifications for their vehicle imports according to Government requirements. New Zealand was one of the few countries with assembly facilities for Morris/Austin vehicles and imported them mainly in "Completely Knocked Down" (C.K.D.) form, while most of the others received the products fully built up.

During this time he gained experience also in the parts warehouse, the claims section and the marketing department where the flamboyant advertisements originated from. He visited most of the factories who were sub-contractors to Nuffield Industries such as Press Steel, who pressed-out all body parts, Lucas Electrical and

the Mowog foundries who cast engine blocks and the like. This was real heavy industry and some people worked under very trying conditions. After that he spent a further six months at various large Nuffield franchises throughout the United Kingdom, slowly working his way through most of their departments where he learnt a lot about service, parts sales and administration which could be utilised later in his career.

On his return journey to New Zealand he went via Flint, Michigan (USA) to attend a Dealer Executive course at the G.M. Institute. This was a marvellous organization for training in all aspects of the Motor Industry, but Ross's course focused mainly on managing large dealerships and financial control. Again, some of their

Mr E.C. Nimon and Jack Porter in 1966.

reporting and accounting systems were eventually adopted at The Dominion Motors Ltd. During his travels fellow students found it hard to believe that the company in New Zealand operated on comparatively small profit margins and volumes, but they were very envious when they heard about New Zealand's Import Licensing Regulations which guaranteed that the company would sell everything it imported! "Used cars were a nuisance to them whereas they were important to us to supplement profits due to small margins and frequent import-restricted production volumes."

On his return to New Zealand in 1961 Ross spent a brief period at the head office in Wellington before he was sent to the Auckland retail branch on a specific assignment for three months. At least that was his understanding. "I arrived with one suitcase only and a bundle of documents—and forty years later I am still here.

In 1965 he succeeded Edward Cecil Nimon who retired after 37 years as Auckland Branch Manager of The Dominion Motors Ltd. From then on he handled all retail aspects for the Auckland City, while Jack Porter took over the wholesale side of the business, overseeing all dealer activities. "This was a real challenge for me to follow-on behind Mr Nimon who had been such a dominant figure within the Company and the Auckland motor industry at large. A man highly respected for his tough but fair dealing and a personality which got the best out of his staff. He gave his best to The Dominion Motors Ltd, but sure expected everyone else to do the same thing.

"The Dominion Motors Ltd was formed in 1919 by the merger of two earlier companies, The Dominion Motor Vehicles Ltd of Wellington, which was founded in 1914 by my Grandfather, Mr Charles Norwood — later Sir Charles — and Mr David Redpath's Universal Motor Company Ltd of Christchurch.

The first Auckland Branch of the newly formed Company commenced business as early as 1919 operating from premises in Myer Street, which is no longer on the map as the site is now the Aotea Centre. The same year, an additional "garage" for the truck and tractor side of the business was secured and altered on the corner of Burleigh and Khyber Pass Roads. A new workshop and service garage was built there in December 1921 and extensions, were added in 1924, 1926, 1928 and 1963. By 1967 the Branch had served its purpose and the buildings were demolished to make room for large concrete water storage tanks intended as the main holding area for Auckland's inner city water supply.

Additional to the Khyber Pass premises of 1919, The Dominion Motors Ltd procured a building on the corner of St. Marks and Great South Roads later known as the "Motordrome", mainly for servicing, undersealing and sales of tyres, batteries and fuel. They also had a small number of used cars on the lot. The same area is currently the home of Coutts Motors Ltd, a Mercedes Benz dealership.

In the mid-fifties it became obvious that the old Myer Street premises were inadequate, that more space and a more upmarket location was required for selling Nuffield Products, leading to the purchase of land on the corner of Broadway and Alpers Ave in 1956. The spacious new building constructed there from April 1957 onwards opened coupled with a big promotion campaign on 1 December 1959, celebrating the Company's 40th anniversary at the same time. The workshop was converted from an old leather factory established in 1945, but the rest of the complex was new, grouping together the executive offices, showroom, parts and servicing departments more or less under one roof. In other words efficiency was the keynote. Commentators at the time described it as "an example of modern commercial architecture of the highest standard."

Above: The first Auckland retail branch established soon after The Dominion Motors Ltd was formed in 1919.
Below: Premises on the corner of Khyber Pass and Burleigh Street, a scene from the mid-1950s.

The Dominion Motors Ltd were the first in the Motor Industry to build in this area which today has become a hub of the modern Servicing and Retail Motor Trade in Auckland.

It would be fair to say that the new Broadway Branch provided a very pleasant working environment for around 145 people and as a result, the dedicated staff continued to turn-in excellent results year after year. The showroom was spacious and light through an imposing frontage of plate glass combined with a high stud. The attractive parquet floor was heated and made it a very comfortable area to do business in. On either side of the showroom floor and at the head of shallow staircases with wrought-iron railings were suites of offices set at mezzanine height. Though there was a great deal of standardisation of office furniture and effects, executives had been allowed to choose their own carpeting. The result was that economical design had been combined with a touch of individuality in each office.

Spare parts were housed in a wall of cabinets behind the showroom floor, and larger ones in the basement directly underneath. About 40,000 different components were stored in neatly classified bins and a few meters away in a room lined with filing cabinets, were the index cards

Interiors of the Khyber Pass branch. Above: A makeshift showroom exhibiting the latest Nuffield products of the 1950s. Left: The workshop, Minors being worked on and a Morris J van in the back-ground; left the cab/chassis is a Morris 5 ton (most likely the petrol version).

upon which a complete record was kept of all spare parts held. As stock was drawn upon or added to, a precise check was made against the appropriate card. A then modern teleprinter-machine kept the Auckland staff in direct and immediate contact with branches in key areas throughout New Zealand. In the event that any part was not held in Broadway, its location elsewhere could quickly be established by consulting other branches and it could then be dispatched directly to where it was required. All

this is quite common today, but those were the days without electronic data processing!

Regarded as one of the most interesting features of the new building was the provision made for waiting customers. A special lounge was set aside for those who wished to wait while their car was serviced. It was well-lit and airy, and the lounge had telephones for the exclusive use of customers. For businessmen it was even possible to carry on the day's work while having their car worked on. They could call upon a

The "Motordrome" in St. Marks Road which later beame the second hand car sales yard. Photo from 1964.

Below: The Broadway Branch show-room in 1959.

stenographer to whom letters could be dictated, and also enjoy coffee or tea—all services were free of charge.

Behind the scenes was a most up-to-date servicing department designed to provide thorough and efficient attention to both big and small repair jobs, as well as routine maintenance. Ross remembers vividly in the early mornings a line of cars queuing from the workshop entrance across the yard onto the road; such was the demand. All vehicles at that time had plenty of grease nipples to fill and oil changes to be made,

much more frequently than is the case today. His fifty-odd staff in the workshop were busy all the time, which made the workflow reasonably difficult to coordinate. In the same place today where the workshop used to be is now a hi-tech equipped, clean-looking Honda servicing department, which reminds Ross more of a laboratory than a service garage. Some of "his" staff were still working for the organization at the time of his last visit, but sadly he learnt that staffing levels in the workshop have been reduced to less than twenty, such is progress.

Press photos used to promote the opening of the new branch with then Branch Manager, Mr Nimon, at right.

Grease nipples are truly a thing of the past, oils and cooling fluids last longer now and service intervals are therefore not so frequent. Engine overhauls are no longer a practical option and consequently no longer done.

In Ross's time at the Broadway Branch a high-pressure car washing machine was at the service of the motorist in a hurry. "I suppose it was an early idea of today's car wash, but still far removed from our modern contraptions. It went on rails forwards and backwards, and squirted water and soap at the car, that was all!" The actual washing was still done by hand as there were no brushes. To the workshop staff it was also very useful for finding water leaks in bodywork which were quite the norm then.

A common feature of some car garages in Auckland, even in the mid-1950s, was the lack of parking space. In the new complex, this problem was virtually eliminated. As well as an

extensive parking area adjacent to the Service Department, there was ample parking space actually on top of the building. A car ramp at the rear lead to a roof car park overlooking the Newmarket district. Another space at one corner of the building was set aside for used car sales.

"The Broadway Branch was the hub of the Northern area maintaining strong rapport with all Dealers from Taupo northwards, who kept us busy. They used to collect their new cars from the Branch as well as being supplied with their spare parts requirements. In hindsight I believe we had too many independent city dealers around Auckland, as there were six of them within 8 miles of the Broadway Branch, and many struggled to survive. These independent dealers actually purchased their vehicles and parts from us and then tried to compete against us in the retail market, a very peculiar situation, but we didn't care how we made our profits,

Mr Nimon's office.

Early days in the showroom

retail or wholesale."

Overall the 63-strong dealer network throughout New Zealand supplied by 7 active branches was one of the major strengths of the organisation and dealers were very well looked after and supported by the head office in Wellington. Some dealerships were just enlarged service centres, but others were quite substantial businesses. The dealers based in rural areas sold and serviced tractors and farm implements as well as cars.

"I recall one of my early tasks as the new Manager was to clear out the strong room, where

I found among other things, a large glass case which housed a magnificent silver trophy which was prepared in 1935 and presented in 1936 by Lord Nuffield to, Sir Charles – then Charles Norwood – and The Dominion Motors Ltd, for being the largest overseas customer for Morris Industries Exports. It was believed The Dominion Motors Ltd was, at the time, the largest single importer of English cars in the world. Despite the fact that the two men were very good business partners, philanthropists, even personal friends, and Sir Charles surely appreciated the award, the trophy was never taken home to Head

Office in Wellington. I proudly displayed it in my office for the duration of my managership and used it regularly as a drinking vessel for champagne to celebrate extraordinary sales results. I now treasure it as a memento.

"The so-called No Remittance Selling gave us additional business and this was where we competed strongly with our opposition. By using funds held overseas, customers were able to obtain an import licence which entitled them to a virtual immediate delivery of a new car, rather than going onto a waiting list. This is the point where our competition came-in as every import licence processed meant an extra car sale. A brief, but exciting period occurred when a member of our Christchurch Branch discovered a means of obtaining qualifying overseas funds through bonus issues of overseas shares. This was legal at the time, but after a rather frantic period of 3 months, during which we processed hundreds of licences, the Government of the day changed the rules and closed it down.

"Successive administrations constantly changed the import licensing regulations, relaxing or tightening imports into New Zealand, a situation that made it difficult to plan too far in advance. At one time the company might be hiring and training staff to cope with increased production and sales, while only a few month later we had to consider reducing staffing levels. Governments also often adjusted duty/sales tax regulations causing major price fluctuations for all. Being wholesalers and retailers we used to be extra busy on Budget nights when the Minister of Finance made his intentions known. I remember selling ten Rolls Royce Silver Shadows in one year during a time when import licensing was relaxed. I am sure this record still stands!

"Since 1949 The Dominion Motors had been importing and assembling the Morris Minor, the Oxford as C.K.D, and for a few years also the Morris Six as fully built up. I believed the Morris Minor to be one of the best designed cars in its class and well ahead of its time for body style, road holding and interior space. The initial Morris Minor Series I, fitted with the old but proven Morris Series E side valve engine, was somewhat under-powered but most reliable. The Minor Series MM fitted with the 803cc Austin designed overhead valve engine proved noisier all round and also less reliable especially when driven harder, which was often the case due to lack of power combined with a bad gear-ratio. As a consequence this model was plagued by crankshaft-bearing and valve-guide problems, as well as gearbox/differential troubles. Oil leaks were standard. The Minor 1000 launched here in 1957 was a much improved car in which you felt very safe as a driver, and because of it, they were often added as the second car in a family. The variants in the form of the 6 cwt van or pick up were very popular for light town work and the Broadway Branch won many municipal and local board tenders with them. We had very good relationships with all sections of the Auckland City Council and Regional Authority, which served us well. In those days business was very personal and it was more important who you knew rather than what you knew, hence we were heavily involved in entertaining.

"I can't recall selling many Tourer Minors, but the Traveller with its wooden exterior frame work was very popular as a No Remittance Import and retained its resale value very well. Both models were imported fully built up only.

"Then, of course, in 1959 came the revolutionary Mini Minor or later just called the Mini in all its variants, which gave us excellent sales for many years. However, the highest volume seller ever must have been the Morris 1100 (later also 1300) as it appealed to private buyers as well as to commercial users. Again, the same as the Mini, this model was ahead of its time with the greatest selling points being the fuel economy, the east-west engine which gave more space in the car, and the hydrolastic suspension which was a real break through in comfort and road holding. Quite common at the time was the so called "badge engineering" in that this model, and others, were produced. Some customers would pay more for a "1100" prestige branded as Wolseley, Riley, MG, or Vanden Plas, while the Morris (or Austin) versions were probably perceived as ordinary, but represented the bulk of our business. The only difference between the cars might have been the front grille/bonnet arrangement and some minor interior changes such as the dashboard layout, the instrumentation or colour schemes. Some models, like the Wolseley or Riley also had twin carburation and free-flow headers to make them a little sportier, which they were, but at the expense of increased fuel consumption and earlier gearbox repairs. Some years later the enlarged 1800cc version proved very popular in the sales initially, but it lacked the power of some competitors in the same class. One of the most exciting cars we had on offer was the Australian designed Leyland P 76 fitted with the Rover V8 engine. It was large, comfortable and stylish with a massive boot. Regrettably the fuel crisis in the 1970s spoilt its chances of success. Over the years we seemed to be continually launching new models: to name a few, Maxi, Allegro, Kimberley, Tasman, Marina and the Nomad.

I think that the B.M.C. would have been more successful if they had fewer, but more reliable models, accruing lower servicing costs. Also in some instances motor performances could have been improved. Overall, however they were good solid cars with generally spacious body shells suited to New Zealand conditions and with the stronger ties in those days to England, we enjoyed a good market share.

In the mid 1960s it became increasingly obvious to the directors of The Dominion Motors Ltd, and other firms on the Austin side of the industry, that it was no longer practical to operate two factions, Austin and Morris, selling virtually the same B.M.C. products just under different badges whilst the international competition, especially from Japan, was getting stronger. This line of thinking coupled with some encouragement from the B.M.C. eventually led to the formation of the New Zealand Motor Corporation in 1969. My uncle, Walter Norwood—later Sir Walter—was instrumental in the negotiations between five major companies that entered into the merger. (Dominion Motors, Magnus Motors, Seabrook Fowlds, David Crozier, P.H. Vickery). Only a few years after NZMC's inception three administrative regions were formed, Auckland, Wellington, and South Island. Our Regional Office was the former Seabrook Fowlds Limited (Austin) building in Symond Street with Mr. John Seabrook appointed to the position of Auckland Regional Manager. Peter Hall, who came from outside of the industry, became Chief Executive in Head Office in Wellington. Many changes were introduced within the corporation over a period of time to strengthen the company in the market against competition from the Japanese and European auto industries. In 1971 the Corporation acquired Amalgamated Pacific Industries, which included the coachbuilding firm Hawke Bros Ltd. One year later the main merger was further consolidated when the New Zealand Motor Corporation bought British Leyland's interests in New Zealand which included the Nelson based assembly plant. The next step—and one of the most important in the history of the group—came in 1976 when the New Zealand Motor Corporation won the franchise for Honda vehicles in New Zealand. I well remember the joy of hearing the announcement which came at a time when British cars were rapidly losing market share, making it hard for us to maintain profits. From small initial volumes, Honda sales soon mushroomed and the vehicles achieved an enviable reputation. Gradually the British products took a back seat and were eventually phased out. From its inception the New Zealand Motor Corporation acquired many other businesses of which some were not related to the motor industry. The business became so complex that in 1981 it was described by its marketing department as a "diversified and expanding manufacturing and marketing group". Officially it was renamed EMCO Group and restructured into three major divisions, which were supposed to reflect its broad areas of activity. There was the NZMC Ltd, the motor division, dealing with the supply, assembly, wholesaling, retailing and servicing of new Honda and Leyland vehicles, and used vehicles. Its retail operation, Motorcorp, was among the biggest automotive retailers in New Zealand with 19 branches nationwide employing more than 700 people, who then sold more than 50 per cent of new Honda and British Leyland vehicles. Motorcorp's workshops took in an average of 500 vehicles a day, for jobs ranging from maintenance to major repairs. I'm not sure if that was a good thing. Then there was Group Rentals Ltd, the television division which had about 34 per cent share in the TV and video market. It employed about 200 staff in 37 branches nationwide. Last but not least is the

This 1956 pick-up is one of the last Series II splitscreen models assembled in New Zealand and fitted with the Auckland-produced Wilco Body which was only available in NZ. It was in long time service for a dairy owner and is still in good condition.

Above: A 1954 Series II saloon seen at a vintage car rally in Greytown. It has since been repainted.

Opposite: This immaculate tourer, a 1955 Series II, UK assembled, is fully restored and takes part in most Morris Minor displays. One notes the period props in the boot (trunk). Here it is pictured at British Car Day in Upper Hutt in February 1999 where it had constant admiration.

8. Rear springs, long semi-elliptic with rubber mountings —piston-type hydraulic shock absorbers.

9 Rubber-backed, deep pile, fitted carpets.

▶ REAR END

1. Luggage boot has over 5 cu. ft. (·15 cu. m.) capacity.

2. Spare wheel is housed separately. Can be reached without disturbing luggage.

10. Rear seat back folds down, leaving unobstructed room right through to the rear of the boot for bulky articles.

3. Separate number-plate light. Twin tail-lights visible from side and rear — an extra safety feature.

4. Full-width one-piece, front and rear bumpers.

Also available to de-luxe specification with passenger's sun visor (Saloons only), heater, bumper over-riders, and seat cushions and squabs leather-covered.

The heater will not be fitted on cars for delivery to overseas territories where it is not applicable. Over-riders are available as an extra on cars to "standard" specification for delivery overseas.

YOUR OWN SALES FEATURES

Produced by The Nuffield Organization and printed by The Nuffield Press Limited, Cowley, Oxford, England. 17/33 (83782) 1/54—5000

MORRIS MINOR
Facts for Salesmen

Your "walk around" sales guide. Starting from the left-hand-side front door handle, we walk round the car in a clockwise direction, pointing out the features as we go.

▶ MAIN SELLING POINTS

1. "Mono-construction." Most modern method of car construction—is stronger, safer, lighter, lasts longer.

2. "Quality First" finish inside and out—degree of finish is remarkably high for price. Six coats of paint, whole body completely rustproofed.

3. Choice of three models— 2-door saloon, 4-door saloon, convertible (lowest priced on market).

4. Modern, pleasing appearance—no awkward curves, not ultra-streamlined. Is a small car with big-car lines.

5. All seats are within the

Publication No. H. & E. 53106

---

wheelbase, for comfort, increased stability and easier driving.

▶ THE FRONT

1. Torsion bar independent front suspension. Permits exceptionally good road-holding and cornering with a most comfortable "ride."

2. Hydraulic piston-type shock absorbers keep the ride smooth.

3. Separate side and headlights. Headlights double-dipping with main beam warning light.

4. 12-volt lighting and ignition system. Constant voltage control.

5. Rack-and-pinion steering. Very light to handle and extremely accurate—good points with ladies.

6. O.H.V. engine gives good cruising and top-gear perfor-

6. Perfect balance—wheelbase, height and track are proportioned correctly.

mance, improved acceleration and hill climbing.

7. S.U. fuel pump and carburetter.

8. Bonnet lock released from inside car. Double safety-catch at front.

9. Engine accessibility good; easy access for routine servicing and maintenance.

10. Good m.p.g. Low overall running costs. Keeps motoring expenses as low as possible.

11. Favourable power/weight ratio. Assists performance and economy.

12. Lockheed hydraulic four-wheel brakes. Easily adjusted.

▶ FOR DRIVER & FRONT SEAT PASSENGER

1. Pleasantly styled facia.

2. Parcel tray right across car. Glove box on passenger's side.

3. Front ventilating windows. Open out to act as air scoops in really hot weather.

4. Driver's sun visor. Friction

mounting holds it securely in position.

5. Front seat backs tip forward and whole seat lifts forward on 2-door saloon and convertible. Getting in and out is very easy.

6. Door hinges are concealed. Outside door handles are flush-fitting, safety type.

7. Warning signal shows when headlamp lights are not dipped.

8. Green warning light tells when sidelights are on.

9. Twin electric wipers.

10. Four-speed gearbox. Gear lever in central position. Positive in action.

11. Cable operated hand brake on rear wheels adjusted automatically at same time as foot brake.

12. Door windows wind fully down.

13. Doors have double-action safety lock—good point with parents of children.

14. With 2-door models children can be carried in back securely—cannot get at door handles whilst travelling.

15. Ashtray in centre of facia panel.

16. A radio can easily be fitted if required.

17. 4-door saloon has interior light.

18. Driver's seat adjustable.

19. Easy car to drive. Small turning circle, compact overall size allow easy parking, garaging and manoeuvrability in traffic.

20. Doors hinged on forward pillars—safety factor if opened inadvertently whilst travelling.

21. Clear driving vision. Slender corner and door pillars eliminate blind spots.

22. 4-door saloon has automatic time control switch for trafficators.

23. Toughened safety glass all round.

24. Sprung steering wheel, horn button in centre.

25. Foot operated dipping switch.

▶ FOR REAR SEAT PASSENGERS

1. Inter-axle seating.

2. Hypoid rear axle. Quiet operation and long life. Permits a low floor.

3. Full-width parcel shelf behind rear seat.

4. Good elbow room and leg room for rear passengers—44 in. (112 cm.) both measurements.

5. Head room ample, consistent with low overall height of car.

6. Convertible rear side windows are permanently fixed. No side screens to stow or crack.

7. 4-door saloon has stainless steel window frames. Arm-rests on rear doors.

This illustration of a 4-door left-hand-drive model was used in European advertising.

UNSURPASSED
IN
ALL-ROUND VALUE

QUALITY FIRST

THE MORRIS MINOR 1000 TRAVELLER

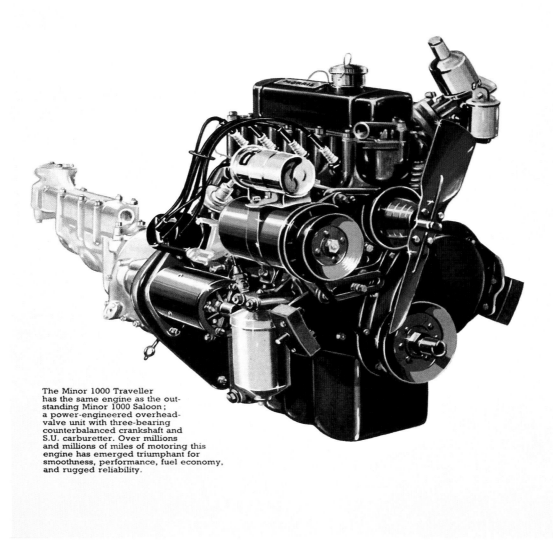

The Minor 1000 Traveller
has the same engine as the outstanding Minor 1000 Saloon;
a power-engineered overhead-
valve unit with three-bearing
counterbalanced crankshaft and
S.U. carburetter. Over millions
and millions of miles of motoring this
engine has emerged triumphant for
smoothness, performance, fuel economy,
and rugged reliability.

Opposite: Advertisements produced in England for the commercial variants. Like the estate car, the vehicles' load carrying capacity was exaggerated.

Left: A fleet of Minor Pick Ups was in sevice for Watties Foods in Hawke Bay. Here a field officer is visiting during harvest time.

Dereliction and splendour.

Left: The main workshop, where vehicles old or new were prepared for the road.

Below: At left the entrance to the basement parts store, in the background the lube bays which were always in demand.

Bottom: Parking wasn't a problem at the Broadway Branch in the 1960s!

Engineering Division comprising three subsidiaries: Hawke Coachwork, designers and builders of coach and bus bodies; Domtrac Equipment (Dominion Motor's tractor and industrial equipment division of 1960) one of the top six suppliers of transport and construction equipment in New Zealand; and Sheetmetal Holdings, specialists in sophisticated fabrication of industrial ovens, heat exchangers and stainless steel products ranging from meals-on-wheels units to fast food equipment.

The image the group wanted to convey to the public was seen as one of the most important aspects. Some of the key operations were given a completely new look in 1982, more in line with modern marketing, and as is usually the case, the design firms had a field day playing around with logos and corporate colour schemes. Eventually, with the NZMC Ltd being a publicly listed company, Honda Japan bought all of NZMC's Honda interests as well as many of its retail branches and dealerships throughout the country. As a consequence our pride and joy, the Broadway Branch, and many others, was virtually demolished in November 1990. A more modern structure was erected in its place within a year, which still represents Honda today.

I had left Broadway Branch in 1980 to become Retail Manager for the seven branches north of Taupo, but then after three years the constant travel became too arduous, and being away from

The Morris Six of 1948, one of Nuffield's less successful vehicles.

home and family for a large portion of the time didn't suit me any longer. Hence in 1983 I decided to go my own way purchasing a parts importing business for European motor vehicles which did well for me and proved to be a good easing off period from the Motor Trade before finally retiring in 1995.

The Auckland Electric Power Board was one of the largest fleet operators in Auckland and took delivery of these 12 Morris 8 cwt vans. Ross George and Sales Manager Mr J.F. Ewart (in the cab) inspect one of them before delivery, photo early 1970s.

Above: The Mini Minor body shell under construction at the Newmarket Assembly Plant in 1964.
Left: The Mini Minor attracted considerable interest from people in the motor industry and the public alike. Chassis only and cut-open cars were displayed in dealerships nation-wide. This display is in the Broadway Branch in 1960.

Jim Stafford, planning engineer (left) and Tom Ayscough, final assembly foreman, cast a critical eye over the first New Zealand assembled Morris 1100 as it came off the line at DML's Newmarket plant on 1 February 1963.

Below: The Riley Kestrel 1100/1300a variant of the more basic Morris model. It featured some cosmetic changes and the dual carbureted engine delivered about 3-4 bhp more, which increased torque. The MG version (left) was quite similar in appearance and performance.

A selection of Dominion Motors' wares on display at a trade show. Yes, they sold Bentleys too!

Above: The former Seabrook & Fowlds Ltd building in Symmonds Street, Auckland, which later became the northern regional office of the New Zealand Motor Corporation.

Right: The Mini or Austin Seven on parade and in showroom display for Seabrook & Fowlds Ltd.

Above: These vehicles, with the exception of the London taxi, were assembled in NZ and marketed under Austin and Morris badges.

Above: The Broadway branch of Dominion Motors Ltd shortly after its opening in 1959.

Right: The same spot in June 2001, now the home of Honda.

CHAPTER FIFTEEN

Stewart Greer Motors Ltd: Dealers

The company initially known as Stewart Nash Motors was founded in 1929 by the late Edmund Stewart, selling and servicing Nash vehicles, and operating a Nash taxi service between the towns of Napier and Hastings. Mr Stewart was a true entrepreneur of the New Zealand motor industry and many folk used to pass compliments as to his skills in selling motor vehicles. Hard work and skill were needed, because starting up in business was tough, the economy was not buoyant and the young firm experienced many difficulties in obtaining sufficient new vehicles even for those few customers who could still afford a car.

Disaster struck the firm when the 1931 Napier earthquake flattened the region. Stewart Nash

Mr Edmund Stewart (above) and Mr W.A. Greer.

Motors' premises were severely damaged and, not long afterwards, the master agency, Nash New Zealand Motors went into liquidation, leaving Mr Stewart with no motor car agency. Soon after he started selling Standard vehicles, but that too was only to last a couple of years before the master agents, Reynolds & Company, went into liquidation.

The 1930s were very difficult years; there were more businesses going broke than there were paying dividends. About this time Stewart Nash Motors were offered the Austin franchise for the Hawkes Bay region, but decided not to take it.

Mr Stewart was a well-liked man who had many acquaintances within the motor industry,

The front of the Dickens Street, Napier, premises.

The tow-truck of Stewart Nash Motors.

some of them dating back to his earliest beginnings in the trade. It was through one of these contacts at Dominion Motors, Wellington, that his firm was offered the Morris franchise for the region. Part of the agreement was that he should open another branch in Hastings in order to increase influence in both population centres. It was then that Mr W.A. (Bill) Greer, Manager of a Motor Garage, was approached to join Mr Stewart in the new venture. The firm grew and its name was changed to Stewart Greer Motors Limited, which it still is today. A new branch was opened in Hastings' Market Street, directed by Bill Greer for the next 25 years or so until his retirement in 1958.

Mr Stewart once told his staff: "The Dominion Motors expect a good dealer to sell a fair share of all their products, we must make every effort to sell all types of commercial vehicles and tractors. Never, of course, forgetting the No-Remittance business. We must always be alert and when given a prospect, don't rest 'till we have made contact and, for preference, secured the business."

Stewart Greer Motors was also very active in the rural scene and this was one of the main reasons for opening a further branch in Waipukurau in 1953, selling and servicing the famous Allis Chalmers tractors, graders, bulldozers and ancillary equipment. These products represented a substantial part of their business in the 1940s. Other principal tractor franchises were for Nuffield, later Leyland, followed by Iseki. Eventually, in 1983, the company decided to sell motor vehicles only.

During the development of Stewart Greer Motors many changes took place, sites were established and later altered according to changing market demands. Buildings were leased, then bought, refurbished and many years later demolished to make room for new innovations. The business founders retired and passed away, the Stewart family sold their interests to the retired Managing Director Len Morley and his wife, and other members sold their shares in the business to relatives in the extended group of families. To cut a long story short, the last of these transactions was in 1996,

Stewart Nash Motors Ltd in Dickens Street, Napier, after the 1931 Hawkes Bay earthquake. The photo was taken by the insurer whose caption read: "Exterior wall useless. Roof on steel frame can be used again. Front recently built is badly cracked."

when Phillip Greer and the Morleys sold their remaining interests to Russell Greer, making him the sole owner and present director of the company. Today Stewart Greer Motors Limited is one of a few ex-Morris franchise holders still trading, selling Honda/Nissan and continuing their 70-odd year dedication to the Hawke's Bay region. They have always led the market in their area and this has many reasons, but the main one is best summarized in the late Mr Edmund Stewart's own words: "Goodwill is the thing, we must all create it, when people are satisfied that we are a reasonable firm and will give them a good deal, then the sale is 90 per cent made."

Above: Morris 8 stock arriving at Napier wharf during the late 1930s. Vehicles were slung off the ship and convoy-driven to the depot, which required all hands on deck, including family members.

Right: The bulk of Stewart Greer Motors's business was with rural customers.

Above: The premises in Napier during the early 1950s.

Left: A popular way of promoting business was the agriculture and trade show, both indoor and outdoor.

CHAPTER SIXTEEN
Watts & Grieve Ltd: Dealers

The central figure in the story of the firm Watts & Grieve is Mr Charles Watts, one of the pioneers of the motor industry in Southland.

Mr Watts, born 1881 in Waimate, grew up to be a remarkable man in many ways. At the age of 10 his parents shifted to Christchurch where he finished schooling and was apprenticed to a local cycle making firm, Adams & Curties, who actually hand-made bicycles. Young Charles learnt his trade well. One of the business partners, Mr Walter Curties, left the partnership to start his own business, taking Charles Watts with him. Together they worked on a new-idea-bicycle which was propelled by long levers with ratchets and a pulley under the saddle. Curties patented his contraption, left for England, and Charles Watts was out of a job. He started at once with the body-building firm of Stevens & Sons, making ironwork for the Christchurch tramcars, but he still had a hankering for the cycle trade and soon returned to the Adams firm. It was about 1896 when he spotted Nicky Oates, a then well-known local cycle dealer, driving along in a Benz car, which impressed him at the first sight.

Charles Watts received the offer of another job with a new firm, Henry J. Ranger Cycle Works, where he enjoyed working for the next nine years. It was through Henry Ranger that Charles Watts had his first "smell of petrol" when a famous cyclist, Bill Martin, also known as "Plugger Bill", of Australia, arrived in the area and, fortunately for Charles Watts, had broken down with his motor-driven tandem pacer. The firm was called in and Charles Watts, who had never laid hands on a petrol engine before, got it going.

Charles Watts, 1881-1956.

This machine required two occupants, one in the front for steering, and one on the back seat manipulating the gears controlling the speed. Racing cyclists used it as a pacer to make the race more spectacular as they strove to overtake it.

The next machine Mr Watts worked on was a Singer Tricycle with two wheels in front and a single back wheel, inside of which was the engine. Awkward, but it was most ingenious! Soon after the pair, Ranger and Watts, launched into the motorcycle manufacturing business using Simms 2.5 h.p. engines, which lead to the making of a three wheel motor car and the agency for Simms & Co. They made about five cars until Mr Ranger became financially embarrassed and the business went into liquidation.

The Bullnose Morris Tourer of 1913.

The early Morris Minor, introduced in 1932.

Mr Watts was introduced to Mr P.H. Vickery of Invercargill, who was wanting a motor mechanic to take charge of his workshop. Charles Watts left Christchurch for Invercargill in 1906 and the first car he worked on was a "Star". Vickery, at that time, had the agency for Humber cars, a well finished product with beautiful paintwork. Later they secured the Renault agency as well.

Motor cars were now becoming more numerous and other makes were coming on the market. With much support and encouragement from his wife, Mr Watts begun business in Invercargill in 1912 going into partnership with Mr Ziza Matthews, giving "service to the motoring public." They called their business the Kelvin Motor Works. The prospects at the time were bright: the Southland Motor Association, in a report, estimated that there were nearly 200 cars in the province and that their membership was steadily increasing!

Two years after the formation of Kelvin Motor Works, Ziza Matthews sold his interests in the business and from February 1914 Mr J. Mort Grieve became the new partner in the firm, which from then on traded as Watts & Grieve. The

KELVIN MOTOR WORKS

WATTS & MATTHEWS

(Late of P. H. Vickery's Motor Department).

Car and Motor Cycle Engineers and Repairers

Clients are Assured of Personal Attention and the Benefit of Our

TEN YEARS' EXPERIENCE WITH ALL MAKES
OF CARS AND MOTOR CYCLES.

NEW AND FULLY EQUIPPED GARAGE

WATTS & MATTHEWS,
KELVIN STREET, INVERCARGILL.

'PHONE—385.   4864

The Watts and Grieve branch in the small town of Gore in Southland, opened in 1936.

The Winton branch in the mid-1950s.

Company's first agencies were for the Phoenix Motor Car and the James Motor Cycle to which Mr Grieve contributed the R.C. Hup Car agency when he joined the partnership. But on demand the firm imported any make or model available. They uncased their first two Morris Oxford 2-seater Roadsters, with the White & Poppe engines, in December 1914, making them one of the earliest Morris dealers in New Zealand. Both cars were sold locally and gave such outstanding service over a number of years, that every endeavour was made to import more, but because of World War I and its aftermath, the Company was unable to procure further supplies until the end of 1924, when further Morris Oxfords shipments arrived.

At this time William Grieve joined the firm as Secretary, new premises were built in Esk Street and the old "Kelvin Motor Works" shop was vacated. In 1926 Mort Grieve sold his shares in the firm and started his own business taking with him the Willys-Overland Agency.

The slump years of the Great Depression (1931–34) brought suffering and hardship to the whole country and, of course, to Watts & Grieve. In 1932 the Company's annual turnover dropped to £19,500 and did not rise above a quarter of what it had been in the previous three years. The same year Watts and Grieve had to give up their status as independent Morris Importers and from then on procured new stocks from The Dominion Motors Ltd who had been appointed sole importer (and later assembler) of Morris vehicles in 1930. Despite the bleak economical outlook at the time the firm tried to increase their influence in the region by opening a second branch in the small town of Gore. The move was most likely encouraged and supported in any way by The Dominion Motors Ltd, as it was generally their policy to help dealerships to get established or expand their business.

By 1934 the firm reported improved turnover in repair work and increased new car sales. The Morris range at that time included the 1932 type Morris Minor, the Ten/Six, Twelve Cowley or Fifteen/Six and the Oxford Twenty. In 1938 the motor business was booming assisted by the Morris 8, but competition was intense and taxation to the utmost. A sudden change in the country's economy occurred just one year later

when WWII broke out and private vehicle sales declined until in 1942 no new or used were sold. Severe import restrictions on petrol and tyres seriously affected the workshop. It became so severe that part of the business had to be closed down. Many staff went into camp.

Two years after the War ended, business started to improve slowly with all Morris 8 and 10 h.p. cars, as well as Morris 25 cwt. trucks sold.

In 1949 the new Morris Minors MM and the new Oxfords MO started to arrive in June and April respectively, and were so popular they considerably increased the demand for cars and created large waiting lists of impatient buyers.

The following is what ex-staff told the author: "When we first saw the Low Lite MM, we were impressed, because the styling of the vehicle was so far advanced to the old Morris Series E, but on closer examination we discovered the torsion-bars, which none of us had seen applied that way, and didn't trust either. But they proved no trouble at all. The 950cc sidevalve engines were good and reliable; you could drive them hard all day, but they were lacking a lot in performance. The car's engine-bay was originally designed to accommodate a flat-four boxer unit which never went into production; this created extra space in the bay which allowed the mechanic to work upside down for better access to the tappet adjusters at the side of the engine block. The car proved to have a very strong diff and a good gearbox; we never had to repair one under warranty. In the Southland region the Minor MM became the most popular of all Morris models available at the time. Watts & Grieve took delivery of Auckland assembled vehicles via the port of Lyttelton (Christchurch) which we had to collect there and drive in convoy of 10-12 cars back to Invercargill. This was usually a job for staff who were not essentially needed at the time. We took our own dealer plates, borrowed more from around the district and travelled to Christchurch by train where the cars were waiting at the wharf ready to drive away. The Sales Manager always instructed us to go slow, 30 m.p.h. until Ashburton (54 miles), increase to 35 m.p.h. to Timaru (48 miles) and 40 m.p.h. the rest (242 miles). But we did not! We'd stop and have a fag and then drove faster to make up time! The demand for new cars was such that on

Above: The Esk Street (Invercargill) branch frontage in 1955. On display (left to right) are: Morris Oxford Series II 1954-56; Magnette Series ZA 1954-56; Oxford MO Pick-up 1948-54; Morris Minor Series II (early) 1952-56. In the showroom window is a Morris J van. Right: The same location 45 years later.

average vehicles had to be collected once a month and the workshop was quite busy accommodating general service work and pre-delivery checks. For that reason they were often done after normal hours, usually at a rate of two cars a night per mechanic who had detailed instructions in form of a checklist to look for things like lose shock absorber mounting bolts, U-bolts, door catches, wheel bolts (or later nuts) and so on.

"Often the cars travelled as deck cargo from Auckland exposing them to a fair bit of salt spray, making paint edges, clips and some chromed steel parts rusty. We'd pick that up in the check too and repair as best as possible, but often they came back under warranty. At this stage we fitted a lot of heaters too."

Towards the end of 1951 large direct shipments of Minor and Oxford cars started to arrive from England, as well as those normally received from the Auckland assembly. Much organization was required to store and get ready for delivery such a large number of cars. The firm was making an impression on their waiting lists at last.

By 1953 the demand for new cars was greater than ever with the introduction of the Morris Minor Series II which resulted in increased waiting lists once again.

The model looked promising in the advertisements, but this is what ex-staff had to say: "The early model's reliability was not repeated in the Minor Series II fitted with the 803cc engine. Customers had lots of problems with it, running the big end and main bearings, probably caused by a deficiency in oil filtration through the use of a by-pass filter and not a full-flow one, as well as the change from Copper-Lead to Babbit White Metal for the bearing shells and the general need to rev the engine higher. Our workshop was constantly busy regrinding crankshafts, fitting under sized shells as well as doing valve grinds and exhaust valve guide replacements, not to mention the near impossible to fix, oil leaks. The gearbox of this model proved extremely noisy in low and reverse which we tried to minimise with a metal treatment called 'Prodregg', that was available then. They also often chipped the teeth in first or reverse. To top it all off, the diffs used to howl in various degrees and really quiet ones were rare. Watts & Grieve had lots of warranty claims on this model creating a bad reputation for the car, so bad that our own rental division refused to have that model."

In 1957 car deliveries improved for a short time, but the introduction of the Minor 1000 and the Oxford Series III increased the demand further. Waiting lists grew long, particularly during 1958 when severe import restrictions combined with high sales and petrol taxes once again curbed car sales. A reduction in sales and petrol tax in 1960 improved trading conditions and the temporary easing of import restrictions allowed in a few more cars. In February that year the new Mini Minor was announced, increasing still further the waiting list for new cars. Severe import restrictions were re-introduced in 1962, but the use of overseas funds for No-Remittance Import Licenses saw a few extra cars imported. Waiting lists, especially for the Minor 1000 and

The Morris Minor 1000 introduced in 1957, a much improved car.

the Oxford were larger than ever that year with some clients having to wait three years before obtaining delivery. The revolutionary Morris 1100 with hydrolastic suspension was announced in August increasing still further the demand for new cars.

Comment from the professionals: "The Minor 1000 was a much improved car in performance and reliability. Overall the car was good in its class, particularly the engines seemed to be lasting longer. The con-rod bearing troubles of the previous model were overcome with larger diameter crank pins and the fitting of Full-Flow oil filters. The gearbox was much improved, but still noisy in low and reverse and the diffs were often wining before high milages were achieved, resulting in complaints and occasionally also in warranty claims."

In 1941 William Grieve had disposed-off his interests and Mr G.C. Tapper, then Sales Manager, took over as Secretary and Director until 1951 when Mr Watts retired and Mr Tapper became Managing Director of the firm. After a brief retirement Charles Edward Watts passed away in his home on 11 April 1956 aged 75 years. Southland had lost one of its foremost pioneers in the Motor Industry and it was mainly due to Mr Tapper's enthusiasm and ability that the business expanded during the next 20 years.

Unfortunately the firm did not prosper much longer after that period. In 1968 the Machine Shop and the Engine Reconditioning Department were sold off and taken over by General Assessory Company. Five years later the Winton Branch was closed and in 1974 followed the Panel Shop. The formation of the New Zealand Motor Corporation created strong competition between its members for a dwindling B.M.C. product market. Many Japanese sourced vehicles were now produced and the demand for Morris and Austin vehicles overall declined. Watts & Grieve's biggest rival in the Southland region, P.H. Vickery Ltd, who had been selling Austin vehicles became a founding member of the new Corporation eventually also making the change to Honda which they still sell today. This development left no market share for Watts & Grieve Ltd, so that directors and shareholders decided in 1978 to scale down the business and, eventually, close shop.

CHAPTER SEVENTEEN

H.J. Jones & Co.: Dealers

Herbert John Jones was born in 1883, was self- educated and up to the stage of starting his own business, worked as an engineer for Ewington's, the Masterton agent for Regal cars. "Herb" became well known in the Wairarapa district for his ability to fix most electrical or mechanical problems that were put in front of him. It seems his name became a by-word among the shearers for his ability to repair the small and unreliable combustion engines that powered the shearing plants at the time. As a general engineer he worked on oil engines, motor bikes and later increasingly on cars. His skill was such that he made a small petrol or gas engine which ran well and was on display for a long time. In 1909 he actually built a small experimental car for himself.

It was 1913 when he commenced his own motor business later known as H.J. Jones & Co. in the town of Masterton working mainly on motor bikes in the beginning, and as numbers increased in the district, also cars. Even though his workmanship always was of the highest standard, jobs were not flowing into the shop in sufficient volume to keep them going. A great deal of work was done outside and in the backblocks. The firm also started to sell a few new cars and among the early ones were two Mighty Michigans, Fiat Zeros and Baby Grand Chevrolets.

One day, Cycle and Motor Suppliers (possibly a general vehicle importer) visited the firm with the first 1913 Morris Oxford Light Car imported into New Zealand. From about 1920 this type of vehicle was known as the "Bullnose Morris Tourer." They were travelling the country promoting the car and at the same time recruiting new agents for the brand. Herb Jones arranged

Herbert John Jones, 1883–1949

to buy this particular car (for his wife apparently) after the tour had finished, which effectively makes him the first Morris owner in this country. He also placed his orders for more Morris cars and was appointed Morris agent for the Wairarapa province.

Soon after that the 1914–18 Great War began and cars were not coming out of England as fast as they could be sold, so Herb reverted back to being a mechanic, tackling the most difficult jobs. Just one of these was making a new crankshaft for a twin-cylinder Darracq car that had broken down. From the time he went into business there was a steady flow of his ex-employer's clients coming to him.

Despite the effects of the war the firm's business grew and the old workshop became too

The first work-shop/showroom in Chapel Street, Masterton. On display from left to right: Hubmobile, Regal, Austin, Krit, Fiat. Photo ca. 1913.

small. In 1916 the firm built new premises in Lincoln Road in the centre of town, gaining additional floor space and a more up-market status, attracting wealthier clientele for their Fiat cars. The extra space in the workshop allowed the assembly of the Chevrolet 490 which were sold in increasing numbers as direct competition to the Model T Ford which did not have electric starters for another two years. From 1916 on the company was known as a "City Garage", but more on that later. Business went well for many years and the firm expanded by adding-on a showroom in 1920 and by opening a further branch in the small town of Pahiatua located about 70 km to the north. The 1930s Depression years slowed business down and this branch was closed again. From the early 1930s the firm H.J. Jones & Co became a dealer of The Dominion Motors' network, selling and servicing the entire Nuffield product range.

Herbert John Jones had four sons, Eric, Leslie, Gordon and Winstone, who from an early age all went into business with him. Eric Jones, the eldest, was Workshop Forman in Masterton until his father's death in 1949 and then became Managing Director until his retirement in 1968. Leslie Jones was Company Secretary and became Managing Director upon Eric's retirement. Gordon Jones and his brother Winstone managed the Featherston Service Garage under the

umbrella of the Masterton business.

Leslie Jones had 50 years of personal involvement with the company that was the second largest motor business in the province. He once explained why the name "City Garage" was given: "In the early days most land owners were really only the wealthy people. They used to take their vehicles to Wellington for servicing in the belief that big city garages gave superior service. So, it was decided to call the Jones' business "city garage", for city-type service. It worked!"

Alan Jones, son of Leslie Jones, who joined the motor business together with his brother Howard in the 1960s, told the author about arrivals of new cars: "The Import Restrictions at the time made business difficult and frustrating, we had plenty of customers on our books wanting to buy, but we just could not get enough vehicles to satisfy the demand. New imported cars were picked up at the Dominion Motors' branch at Kent Terrace in Wellington and driven nearly 100 km to Masterton, while vehicles from the Auckland assembly came to us directly by train, something like 3–4 at a time made up an average assignment. Collecting them at the rail yard was not a job people volunteered for and more often than not family members had to help out. The rail workers in Auckland used thick hemp rope to secure the vehicles, tractors and

The new premises in Lincoln Road, Masterton, about 1916.

implements onto the flat-deck wagons. Usually the knots pulled tight and got wet as well so it was almost impossible to undo them. In the early years vehicles travelled open and unprotected on the wagons pulled by steam locomotives resulting in oily soot deposits on the cars' paintwork. After diesel locos were used they got covered in diesel smut. In time NZR introduced heavy rail covers which proved to do even more paint damage until they protected the cars first with a soft cover, which was too useful to return. Fully built-up imports from the UK were usually not boxed at all and travelled in the ship's hold or sometimes as deck cargo exposed to salt water. For that reason they were covered in a protective coating which was hard to wash off, even with kerosene!"

The Featherston Service Garage closed in 1974 and the Head Office of the firm H.J. Jones & Co. closed in late 1979. Franchises held by the company at various times over the years included Hudson, Essex, Fiat, Chevrolet, Packard, Dodge, Morris, Austin, Bentley and Rolls-Royce. In 1980, when the company was sold to Tullochs, a local farm machinery dealer, the main franchise was Honda. Shortly after that the business had a change of name to Motorco and in 1986 the

Honda franchise moved to Southey's Autoworld. Tullochs closed the Lincoln Road business as a motor garage.

Terry Beresford lived in Masterton for over 50 years, was associated with members of the Jones family, and was a customer of H.J. Jones & Co. for many years. He remembers: "In 1955 my father, Alfred Beresford, bought a second hand 1952 Morris Minor two-door, which was already the high-light version, but still fitted with the sidevalve engine. He used it for his day to day requirements. About twelve months later my father was reading a British newspaper that a relative had posted out and in doing so he spotted an article about a new 10 h.p. Morris Minor that would be released at the end of the year in England. This news was most interesting to him as he had always said that the Minor was under-powered and it spoiled the car. Dad was most enthusiastic and he and I talked about the idea of such a car for the rest of that Sunday.

"The following day he paid a visit to the local Morris dealer, H.J. Jones & Co, in Masterton to place an order for the new model. 'What 10 h.p. Morris Minor?' was the reply from the Sales Manager who knew nothing as yet about such a car. The following day my father returned with

Lord Nuffield (left) greets Herbert Jones on one of his visits to Masterton in February 1939.

the newspaper and was then promised the first four-door model that they received. As good as their word, one year later the Company notified my father that his new Morris Minor 1000 had arrived and would be ready for collection in two days time. The exact date was 30 July 1957.

"This Morris Minor 1000 was not the first new model to come to our province of Wairarapa as there were a pair of two door Minor 1000's sold in Masterton before dad's arrived, however, it was the first four-door. When he arrived home with the new car he was told by my mother Elsie

to take it back as she did not like the 'loud' colour which was called 'Field Green.' It bordered on lime green and was very bright for its day. My father replied that this was a safe colour for the road and urged my mother to put her shoes on and come for a ride. All four of us (I have an older brother) were very excited about the car which drove like a sports car compared to the earlier model, and as we found out later, was much more economical too! Mum and Dad had friends in Cambridge [New Zealand] and over the next few summers we would drive there for

The Lincoln Road premises photographed in the early 1960s.

holidays. Always, for several days after the journey, dad would brag about the qualities of his special car, especially the fact that 'she' did forty-six miles to the gallon on long runs. This was proved many times.

"After my father's death in 1973, aged seventy-three years (my brother and I had long since left home) there was only one thing for me to do, and that was to teach my seventy-year-old mother to drive. After all. she still needed to get about town. The Minor had only 23,283 miles on the clock and was still like new. Mum was as keen as I was to keep the car in the family, so the lessons started. The first step was to take mum to the local aerodrome where there was plenty of space, and where it would be 'safe'. After several visits there she handled the gears and all the rest of driving quite well, considering her age. At the end of one of her lessons at the aerodrome I asked mum to drive right on the edge of the mown airfield. At thirty miles an hour she was keeping a good straight course about six inches from the long grass when out of the corner of my left eye I saw movement. As we passed by, up popped two heads looking very surprised! We had almost run over the legs of a pair of lovers lying in the grass. We were as shocked as they were.

"My mother drove the Minor for the next eleven years, but in 1985, and now over eighty years old, she gave it up. The car was passed-on to my brother and myself. After a discussion with him I agreed to pay him half of the value of it and it was then given to my wife June. The car by now had 27,560 miles on the clock and was still in very good condition!

"Today this car is a family heirloom in a real sense, and at 64,200 miles [103,300 km] is still in remarkably good condition for its age. The cylinder head has not been removed since it was new and to date only the exhaust system, clutch and brakes have been the only major parts renewed. Over the years only the front mudguards have suffered some minor blemishes and been touched up, but all the rest of the paintwork is original. The car is still in regular use around town.

"Yes, this Morris Minor 1000 is still something special and we will never see the likes of it again. Thank you Lord Nuffield!"

Mrs Elsie Beresford on the day she passed her drivers licence test in 1973.

Terry and June Beresford in 2000 caring for CJ2680 long after the original owners have passed on and the company which supplied it has vanished more than two decades ago.

Stickers like this one were placed on the dash of every new car sold.

CHAPTER EIGHTEEN
Economy Run

ere follows the text of a press report from 1955:

"There seems nothing very spectacular about the progress of forty-odd stock cars travelling at somewhat sedate speeds over 700 miles of ordinary road between Wellington and Auckland. Yet, when forty-three cars did just that in late November in the Mobilgas Economy Run, over a thousand people, including the Minister of Transport, turned out to see them leave, and hundreds lined the streets of the towns through which they passed. Tens of thousands more listened to broadcast progress results each night or read the progress story of the event in the daily press.

Something about this Economy Run must have caught the public's attention for the interest in it was nothing short of phenomenal and certainly exceeded the oil company's fondest dreams. To identify that element which attracted the person-in-the-street is not difficult. New Zealand is on a per-capita basis the second most highly motorised country in the world with a motor vehicle to roughly every family. This meant that a very large percentage of our adult population was directly interested in the results of the event. Furthermore, this was not a race requiring expert skill and rare courage. Nor was it a reliability trial to put cars on the rack of unformed roads and treacherous bogs. This was a test in which any average motorist could enter with a fair chance of success and it produced results which interested people in a place where everyone's interest is exceptional—the pocket!

Emphasis on stock cars, average driving

It was to the credit of the sponsors, and the Association of New Zealand Car Clubs which controlled the event, that strong emphasis was placed on the "stock" nature of the cars and on

the average driving conditions which the route involved. They did meet mobs of sheep and cattle; the roads were certainly 'under repair' in the Tongoporutu and Awakino Gorge areas; there was plenty of 30 m.p.h. driving in built-up areas with two alert observers to note any movement of the speedo-meter needle above the vital mark. The fact, too, that, before the event began, the Board of Stewards had ruled conclusively on such points as overdrive and standard fuel (no 'two-stroke' mixture) meant that there were no annoying protests after the run to detract from its credibility in the eyes of the public.

"Officially a 30 minute protest period was allowed from the time the results were officially posted. Not only were no protests received in that period, but no questions were asked by those drivers who saw penalties against their names on the results board. In one case this meant the loss of £100 prize money for an entrant who had slowed to a crawl, but not to a halt, at a compulsory stop sign. Purists might complain that a 4 a.m. start is not "average" motoring (though we might find our roads a little less crowded in holi-

day times if more motorists took advantage of the dawn). However, early starts were essential to allow the cars to complete the second day's run in daylight and to arrive in Auckland by midday on the final day. He would be hypercritical who would cavil at this aspect of what seemed to the competitors a miracle of organisation.

"All of those experienced in competitive events in New Zealand were unanimous in voting the run the best organised stock car event yet held in the country.

"Organisation problems

The organisational work behind the economy run was exacting. Finding two hundred beds in Palmerston North meant using fifteen hotels and waking all participants at 5 a.m. Yet all of them were enjoying a hot breakfast at 5.30 a.m. Cars and competitors and observers had to be brought from all over New Zealand and moved home again. Reams of tickets and stationary were used in the travel and accommodation arrangements alone.

GATHERING of all the cars for the forthcoming Mobilgas 700-mile economy run to Auckland in Taranaki Street today. After three days of checking and tuning, the cars are due to leave Wellington on Thursday.

"Checking 46 cars for conformity with stock standards was another king-sized job, yet the Chief Scrutinizer, John McMillan, and his associates, managed it in three days as did the team who gave every car a complete 5000 mile check. Levelling and fuelling procedures were impressive, as was the accuracy with which the results were calculated. One criticism of the fact that the results were calculated to the fourth place of decimals is completely answered when it is realised that the petrol was dispensed to the nearest fluid ounce (.00065 of a gallon). In the ton-miles-per-gallon formula, the weight of the car and occupants is multiplied by the distance travelled and then divided by the petrol used. If the petrol is calculated to the fourth decimal place, then in the interests of accuracy so should be the final result. To give point to this, the placing in the big sweepstakes section (for which the second prize was £100) found only .011 separating second and third cars.

"Sensible driving–no dawdling

Equally impressive were the results of the run from both the mechanical reliability and the road safety viewpoints. Forty-three cars began the run; one dropped out on the first day because of a fault in the cooling system. The only other mechanical troubles were an oiled-up plug and a broken muffler bracket—and the car with the plug trouble still won its class.

"The 42 cars which completed the distance travelled over 30,000 miles without so much as a scratch on their paintwork. They abided by every rule of the road safety code and prompted the Transport Department's Road Safety Officer, Mr A.J. Edwards, who travelled on the run, to state: 'The standard of driving was superb. If most drivers handled their cars as carefully and as well, a good many of our safety problems would be solved.'

"The Economy Run was no easy amble as one driver, Mr S.V. McEwen, noted in his impressions of the run published in *The Dominion*: 'There was no time for dawdling,' said Mr. McEwen, 'a time limit for each day's run making it imperative for all competitors to cruise [where road standards permitted] about 45 m.p.h. It proved you can make good time if you keep rolling.'

"Generally, that was the impression of all contestants. You could not waste time but you could drive safely and sensibly and still maintain a reasonable average speed.

"Driving techniques

Several competitors drove with their shoes off for better 'feel' of the accelerator pedal. All of them avoided 'revving' the engine unnecessarily, es-

ECONOMY-RUN CARS READY FOR BIG TEST

SCENE in Wakefield Street today when cars for the 700-mile economy run to Auckland were all ready for this afternoon's start.

pecially in starting where the smooth get away, if slower, was more economical than the 'jackrabbit' start.

"They got into top gear quickly and kept there on hills until the needle dropped back to about 25 m.p.h. They used the choke sparingly and avoided sudden speed-ups. Most important, they looked ahead and cruised comfortably instead of rushing up to obstructions and standing on the brakes, as do most drivers. In other words, they were patient, pleasant motorists.

"The 'shrewd-heads' weren't able to use their wind-screen wipers except when it was essential as it has been found that the vacuum type wiper makes the mixture a little leaner and so improves consumption. Tyre pressures were standard, as were crankcase, transmission and differential oils and wheel-bearing grease.

"And the tune-up facilities were the same as are available to the average motorist. So typical in fact, that there was a bad moment at the starting line when too lean a mixture kept one car stationary for some seconds.

"That, the officials insist, was not the only bad moment—certainly the 3 a.m. reveille at Rotorua was not the most cheerful time on the trip—but whatever the backroom headaches, the organisation proved excellent for competitors, observ-

ers and spectators alike; the Standard-Vacuum Oil Company (NZ) Limited had every reason to feel satisfied with New Zealand's first and highly successful Mobilgas Economy Run.

"The 'pay-off" for the trade

The Company prepared a leaflet for distribution by service stations and garages called *How to Get More Miles Per Gallon with Mobilgas*. It answered the questions which might be asked by motorists as to how the economy run cars chalked up such astonishing figures. It explained that sensible driving and proper tuning are indispensable allies of quality petrol if economies in petrol consumption are to be achieved. It encouraged the motorist to ask his service station or garage for a 'top' tune-up.

"It is here that the 'pay-off' lay for the retail motor trade in that the Economy Run should make motorists more conscious than ever of the need to keep their engines tuned to a proper pitch. The trade cannot drive the cars for their customers, but they can cash in on a greater awareness among car owners of the importance of engine performance. *How to Get More Miles Per Gallon with Mobilgas* is one leaflet that everyone should be eager to distribute."

CHAPTER NINETEEN

Laurie H. Cromie: recalling Economy Runs

About 1950 in the USA the Mobil Oil Company introduced the idea of running a contest between the major motor-car manufacturers to prove to the public what the American cars of that time would achieve in miles per gallon. It was an era of gasoline promotions with Texaco touting, then Power Chief and most other oil companies following with their own various products.

In a controlled rally contested by the leading manufacturers and sponsored by Mobil Oil the win by the eighteen weight cars of Studebaker and Rambler soon showed General Motors, Ford and Chrysler that they too had better get into the act and refine their old heavy side valve engines and improve their new OH valve engines now coming on stream.

Customer loyalty was still the big factor in the USA when buying a car, but it became a selling point if your Chevrolet or Ford was able to nearly keep up with the light weights.

It became apparent that the annual Economy Run had become a marketing tool for both, the vehicle manufacturers and the petrol companies, so the idea was mooted to extend the competition to Europe, Australia and New Zealand. That way

not only the idea of an Economy Run was brought to this country, but also the brand "Mobil" was introduced in October 1954, taking over from "Plume" which had been selling here for 40 years.

"New Mobilgas is not just another higher octane petrol. It is an entirely new kind of petrol. Mobilgas has been specially developed to overcome current engine problems and to provide you with a new experience in motoring pleasure and performance… it's the finest, most complete petrol ever made available to the New Zealand public!"

The first Mobilgas Economy Run went from Wellington to Auckland over 24–26 November 1955 and was won by an MG Magnette on a ton/miles formula. Good performances were

returned by the 'A' class cars in actual miles per gallon, the Standard 8 & 10 HP, the Morris Minor 803cc and the Austin A30. In class 'B' the Volkswagen Beetle and Ford Prefect did well, and in class 'C' Vauxhall Velox and Standard Vanguard were the leaders. The cars fitted with an SU carburettor showed their superiority in every class.

The following year Mobil decided to really go for the idea and set out to run the biggest event on roads in New Zealand. The 1956 Mobilgas Economy Run was to begin in Invercargill on day one via Lumsden and Gore to Dunedin. Day two ran from Dunedin to refuel at Rakaia and then to Lyttelton. Loaded onto slings onto the vessel *Rangitira* all 35 cars were stowed on the deck and unloaded next morning at the port of Wellington. Day three ran from Wellington via Palmerston North to Rotorua. Day four started early in Rotorua and finished at noon in Auckland. The journey was around some 950 miles (1530 km).

News coverage was extensive; radio reports were broadcast nearly every hour and crowds lined the small town streets to see the cars go by. Money was no problem to the organisers of the event and the prize giving ceremony and dinner was lavish… a real eye opener to a country boy from Rakaia, like Laurie. The first prize was £500 and as mentioned went to the MG Magnette, which was almost guaranteed under the ton/miles formula. The drivers that year were selected from skilled rally drivers and members of car clubs who entered their own cars into the ballot for starters. Few motor distributors were interested in giving or lending their newest model to participate in a "car rally". Laurie's '55 Chevrolet, 6 cylinder Blue Flame engined,

returned 26.5 m.p.g., a good ton/miles figure but not up to the MG Magnette's 45 m.p.g. — "I had a lot to learn!"

In 1957 Mobil decided to accept for ballot any person who entered, and while they got some very skilled drivers, they also got a few who had a new car, but needed driving lessons. This run resulted in a couple of accidents, fortunately not serious. One car hit the entrance of a road tunnel and another had a small collision at an intersection in New Plymouth. This confirmed Mobil's intention to return to skilled drivers from car clubs.

The 1959 Mobilgas Economy Run went from Blenheim via Christchurch, Oamaru, Queenstown, Invercargill to Dunedin. Laurie entered his new 1959 Ford Prefect, but with its 100E Side Valve engine was no match for the Morris Minor… more lessons to learn!

In 1962 his friend Fred Richard persuaded Drummond & Etheridge of Ashburton, a very fine member of Dominion Motor's dealer network, to lend them a new '62 Morris Minor to participate in that year's Economy Run. Fred had been a very good client of theirs since the war and had no trouble getting the car and

everything else they wanted. The Minor had only done about 4000 miles, was registered in the name of the firm and used presumably by Mrs Drummond. Four weeks before the event Laurie was able to strip the engine, change pistons to high compression which guaranteed an extra 4 m.p.g. He re-used the oil rings and the second compression rings from the old pistons, but put new top compression rings in. The parts were all standard and available from a registered dealer, as was required by the rules of the competition. They set the battery voltage as low as was permitted, to decrease the load on the dynamo, that way the battery would obtain its voltage quicker and would be charging for a lesser period of time. There was no point in using special oils or greases because Mobil refilled and greased the cars with their own products. Never the less, attention to detail was the name of the game in preparation for the Mobilgas Economy Run. The event started from Nelson via Westport, Greymouth, Lewis Pass, Christchurch to Dunedin, it was done in 1–2 hour legs and lasted five days, from Monday to Friday. Fred was the nominated owner/driver of the car and Laurie was the nominated co-driver, but according to the rules they had to share the driving equally, changing drivers at every stop. A referee in the car would ensure they follow the rules and he

The team spotted here in their Morris Minor passing through Hanmer.

kept a log on how far each of us had driven. The person who was short of mileage nearing the end had to do the last lag. Fred was a good driver and one of the best navigators, he had been trained as a navigator in a Stirling Bomber in World War II. and had lots of experience in local economy runs held by the Ashburton car club. Laurie's skills covered rally driving, speed events, and a considerable range of mechanical knowledge which he gathered as a supervising flight mechanic working on Corsair aircraft during the war. They were a good team, never in danger of defeat in a good Minor 1000.

That year, 1962, the ton/milage formula was abolished and the actual m.p.g. was the only result of interest to the public. For the preparation leading up to the event they decided that they would use a petrol meter to test the car and learn how to drive on the flat or the hills to obtain the optimum miles per gallon. Drummond & Etheridge lent them a Zenith petrol meter of 1920s vintage that had a half pint glass pipette which had a 3-way control tap. While running at a steady 45 m.p.h. (72 km/h) Laurie would fill the glass to the measure line and when ready would switch to "run", read the Speedo and at the same time start his stop watch. When the

petrol level reached the lower mark he would read the Speedo again, stop the watch and record the distance against time. Cutting two seconds off the elapsed time would decrease the miles per gallon achieved by more than 1 mile per gallon. They found that going slightly uphill or downhill on the Canterbury Plains had a great effect too and they studied the direction of the wind to assess its effect on them. During testing and the actual event the car's windows were always closed to minimise drag, so they had to rely on outside clues for wind direction, things like grass and trees bending to the wind. During these observations they also learnt that sheep always stand with their tails to the wind. Of course they could not plan for every possibility, a certain amount of good fortune was needed too. For example stock hazards were common, a farmer might be shifting 4000 sheep in front of the car and one had to let them trickle past; possibly most of the competitors would strike that as well. "In a different situation you might be lucky, travelling at 50 m.p.h. and just ahead of you is a truck going your speed. Drivers were not allowed to tail-gate, but there is an advantage even if you are 50 or 80 yards away. The referee would be pretty conscious of how close you were and after a little discussion you were told to back off, but we certainly rode the rules as far as possible," Laurie recalls.

The need for a more accurate assessment prompted Laurie to make another petrol meter which could be used on shorter distance tests. It had a 500cc glass measure and also a 200cc vertical calibrated glass as an alternate measuring device. With this they could fill 30cc in the glass and see how far they managed to climb a hill from point A to B in each gear with the time recorded. "We found that, to achieve the greatest economy against time spent en route, it was necessary to try and use constant revs and change down quite soon on a climb. Final figures showed that we could get 45 m.p.g. at 45 m.p.h., 50 m.p.g. at 40 and 40 m.p.g. at 50 m.p.h. The conclusion was that 5 miles per hour was worth 5 miles per gallon. We always bettered these figures on the actual event due to concentrations on every point on the road." Refuelling stations were set up at nearly every Mobil garage along the route for promotional reasons and every contestant was compelled to take on a minimum of half a gallon of fuel or any quantity after that. Most cars that stopped at the first refuelling point took on a gallon, or more if they really needed it.

"We took on a gallon and a half, which was more than we actually needed. When we got to the second refuelling point, which also was a check and final for the day on which the results came out on, our class competitors were reading our pump and came to a wrong conclusion. At mealtime one of the drivers came over to ask us if we had worked out our average miles per gallon for today. 'No not really,' was my laid back answer, and he replied 'but *we* did … 72 m.p.g.!' It was a trick, we did in fact only 50 m.p.g., but it got them worried until the official results came out later. During the next lag this competitor made several costly mistakes through being upset. Much later he told me having not slept that night. These mind games worked for us more than once and I enjoyed playing them to the max.

" The fact that we prepared ourselves mentally and studied every thing that affected fuel economy, spark timing, tyre condition, mixture and recorded results on a graph sheet, gave us the confidence that our Morris Minor would not only win our class, but also overall, as it would regularly return us 50-55 m.p.g. It was not sufficient for us 'just' to win, but our goal was by how much. This time the Minor returned 52.5 m.p.g. and won the class and overall!

"In the 1963 Mobilgas Economy Run we approached the contest from a different angle. This time I joined forces with George Drayton. There was offered by Mobil a grand prize in form of a cabin cruiser and money if any one could guess the results of the four classes. We made up a team to win all four classes, we hoped. There was Eric Wilkinson in a Standard Vanguard with overdrive in class 'D', a Sitter. In class 'C', I entered a Vauxhall Victor 1500 hoping my skill would turn the tide. In class 'B' we had George

On its way to victory the Morris Minor 1000 motors through Lewis Pass. The other vehicle belongs to an official observing and the radio reporter is preparing an update item for the hourly broadcast of the event.

Laurie Cromie's home-made petrol meter specically mounted for these shots onto the passenger door of an abandoned Morris Minor discovered at Christchurch Airport where the author interviewed Laurie.

The mayor of Hamilton flags away the Morris Minor on the 1961 economy run.

After the event the winning Morris Minor was displayed in Dominion Motors' dealerships throughout the country. This picture was taken in the Christchurch show-room.

Laurie Cromie (left) and Fred Richard, the winning team of 1962.

Drayton in a new Morris 1100, who was expected to be the winner. In class 'A' we entered a Renault Dauphine 850cc, a regular loser all over the world. The odds of any one else choosing these four would be zilch.

I spent a lot of long hours on preparing the Renault and teaching the drivers how to drive for economy in a 3 speed 850cc. The '63 Dauphine had been improved by the manufacturers with a new style Zenith carburettor and Michelin tyres which were worth 3 m.p.g. My Vauxhall Victor should have been a 1600cc 4 speed, but came on loan as a 1500cc with a 3 speed box. I was hard pressed to improve it much."

The event started in Wanganui, ran around Mount Egmont to New Plymouth and back to Wanganui. The Renault Dauphine had a charmed run all day to finish with 56 m.p.g.. No other class 'A' car did so. The Morris 1100 led his class closely ahead of the next, the Victor placed third and the Vanguard won his lead in class 'D'.

"During the following day the Dauphine seized her second gear onto the shaft on the trip around Mount Ruhapehu and we had to work feverishly in the lunch hour to free it. Fortunately the

bottom plate of the gearbox came off and we were able to strike the gear with a hammer and punch. It appeared that the gearbox had been refilled with ordinary 30W oil instead of EP90 when the Mobil garage serviced the car before the start line." This cost the Dauphine some m.p.g. on this lag but after that everything went OK and the team John Cornelius / John Stubbs 'ran away' with the class 'A' grand prize.

George Drayton secured his win in class 'B', but only just. "I was not able to overhaul a Fiat 1500 on the final day and was much disappointed when during refuelling the operator spilt my petrol fill. I lost by .002 m.p.g. ! So much for class 'C'."

The class 'D' was won by Eric Wilkinson in his Vanguard as we predicted, and a ten year old

boy won the cabin cruiser. When asked why he chose the Dauphine, he said, "My grandmother owned one!"

"In the 1970s the Economy Runs' petrol consumption was measured electronically, but still confused by influences such as day temperature, fuel temperature, engine temperature and battery voltage. The Oil Company always started the first day's run fuelling the cars early in the day and finishing the event about noon. The coefficient of expansion of fuel for every degree centigrade would skew the result in the Oil Company's favour and grant them a free advertising coup.

Finally it became obvious to us that there was more to be gained by tuning the driver than spending too much on tuning the car!"

CHAPTER TWENTY

Kevin Fisher: Collector

Kevin first became involved with Morris Minors during his apprenticeship as a panel-beater in the early 1960s when he was involved with repairing them for the Auckland Gas Company, the Power Board and many smaller private firms. These big companies operated large vehicle fleets—mostly Minor vans—for their service personnel. The vehicles generally had a tough life as they were constantly loaded to the max with equipment or materials and during their 100,000-mile (161,000 km) lives became regularly involved in small accidents. Those in the panel shop kept most front panels, such as the radiator grille, bumper and guards pre-painted in the organization's respective colours, ready to bolt on. In that way they completed on average one vehicle per day.

Many years later Kevin's girlfriend at the time owned a Morris Minor which he restored for her. Both of them had an interest in these cars and they joined the Morris Minor Club of New Zealand. Other club members admired Kevin's restoration work and gave him plenty more to do, which in time got him professionally involved again. He also joined the club's committee and later was elected its president.

In 1981 Kevin started his own panel-beating and restoration business in Auckland, under the name of "Morris Minor City", specialising in quality body repairs and mechanical modifications of the car. From the beginning his motto was: "If you want the job done right, come here, and if you don't, stay away!" Customers did just that and over the years he spent a great deal of time correcting other people's botch-ups.

In the early years he did a lot of conversions fitting Datsun 120 Y engines and running gear, trying to bring the vehicle up to a more acceptable motorway speed. Morris Minors were still plentiful on New Zealand's roads then, even in Auckland, and they were more often than not driven as every day cars. Business was going well at that time so in 1987 Kevin visited the Morris Minor Centre in Bath, UK, to gain an insight of their operations and to bring a container load of new panel parts back to New Zealand where certain stocks were no longer supplied by the agent, the Motorcorp (retail division of NZMC).

Since the early 1990s, however, the lower end of the automotive restoration market has declined sharply. Reasons for this are the much tougher Warrant of Fitness regulations and the VIN (Vehicle Inspection Number) which presents a costly process, and stringent testing in the case of lapsed registration. Other factors are the availability of relatively cheap and more

Kevin's workshop with some clients' cars. Kevin himself has a collection of 16 immaculate Minors.

comfortable Japanese second-hand car imports in New Zealand and the always unfavourable exchange rate between the NZ Dollar and the Pound Sterling. Over the last ten years UK prices have risen also, while the average income of New Zealanders has stagnated or even declined, making most part imports and the shipping thereof a very expensive exercise. Regardless of how much sentimental value a Morrie has for its owner, in most cases the question of keeping it roadworthy or not has become a financial issue. If the cost of a proposed restoration exceeds the perceived market value of this model, then most owners will not go through with the project, especially when the dreaded body rot usually

pushes the cost of a full rebuild up and above the NZ $5000-10,000 mark, with no difficulty at all! "The combination of all these factors, I'd say, has eroded away about 90 percent of Morris Minors in the Auckland area, and many other English post war classics in the same class as well," Kevin says.

"Of course, there will always be the small group of enthusiasts like myself, who are prepared to invest heavily in order to keep their cars in sound condition, but as a matter of fact the pool of Morris Minors 'on the road' is constantly going down, and I fear that a specialised business like mine will be no longer viable in this form in the very near future."

Kevin's 1971 Morris Minor Van which he uses to commute to work and for all requirements of his business, Morris Minor City. He believes that this one is the tidiest van in New Zealand.

Left: A conversion to disc brake, one of Kevin's own developements.

Below: A Japanese diff and a Morris diff (right) which Kevin has adapted and fits to the axle.

CHAPTER TWENTY- ONE

Ian Hope: Collector

From zero to over 300 in 15 years, that is Ian Hope's record: not in terms of kilometres per hour, of course, but in collecting British cars. When the author visited Ian for the first time in his private museum in Te Awanga, near Hastings, he was eager to present his collection and spoke about a couple of "new" cars he had purchased just the previous day and one or more he was going to look at the next. Three years later when telephoned for an update, he made similar remarks. Ian had just returned from another shopping trip and was about to add to his already impressive collection of retired British motor cars. He is serious about saving them all, no doubt about it!

Ian Hope, an energetic sixty-year-old, grew up in Gisborne, trained as a mechanic and opened his own service garage near Hastings which he operated for almost 10 years. When the storage tanks eventually needed upgrading and the fuel company did not want to "come to the party", he decided to change his career and look for other things to do. During the next 9 years he worked without holidays buying and upgrading several rental properties in the Hawke's Bay area, an investment strategy that now provides him with a modest living as well as financing his hobby, the museum.

The events leading up to the collection began unbeknown to Ian in 1968 when his uncle bought a '62 Morris Minor for his wife. The car was in regular use until the couple had passed away in 1986. Ian restored it for his first great niece and intends to look after the gift until she comes of age. To date Ian has 17 great nieces and nephews, who all eventually will receive a Morris Minor out of his collection. From such humble beginnings the collection soon grew too big to

be housed in sheds and garages dotted around the district so Ian purchased a modern, disused fruit packing shed. This he extended and doubled in floor space to 3600 square metres. The building consists basically of two halves, the storage/workshop area where the new arrivals are given an overhaul, and the now even further enlarged showroom which displays the main collection, including about 30 Morris Minors who take centre stage. Most vehicles' registrations are on hold, that way they keep their present number plates, even thou they are not taxed for road use. Most of them will start up after been given fresh fuel and a battery, Ian assures me, and having myself tinkered on British cars for 15 years I find that quite believable. The interior walls of the shed including a mezzanine floor are decorated

with all sorts of relicts ranging from road signs and number plates to photographs, books and badges, all related to more romantic days of motoring in New Zealand. Nearly all vehicles, about 200 have been bought locally as they became available in the Hawke Bay area. Approximately 50 cars have been donated by owners who wanted a good home for their faithful friends and they obviously very much appreciated the idea of such a museum.

As nice as it all might sound, not all people in the area are supportive of the idea. Despite the fact that Ian Hope has already complied with a number of ever so niggly regulations, and the museum's grounds are clean and tidy, local authorities have made his life difficult since the day he started operations. At the time of writing he has not been granted a full consent to operate as a business until he provides 36 car parks (plus 2 extra for handicapped drivers), also seals the driveway and establishes hedging to hide all of it. These requirements are costly and the museum at this point is hardly profitable! Can the authorities not see that this man's sole effort helps to preserve a large part of this country's motoring heritage and also has a spin off for the local economy by attracting additional numbers of visitors into the area? Words fail!

CHAPTER TWENTY-TWO

Jim Speers: Collector

rive through the gateway of Jim Speers' 25-hectare farm near Hastings and you instantly realise where his allegiances lie, at least in terms of giving refuge to old machinery. The driveway is lined with about a dozen obsolete agricultural implements that date back to the earliest days of farming in New Zealand, and as you progress down the drive you enter a small village made up of corrugated iron sheds, lean-to's and barns of all sizes and descriptions. Most of these buildings which are not essential to Jim's Lucerne hay business are filled to the point of bursting with vehicles, ranging from pre-war tractors and crawlers to vintage or classic motorcars. Some vehicles could even be classed as modern. It is quite obvious however, that the majority of the older cars are Morris Minors. A Shangrila for the enthusiast! Don't get the impression that all this is unordered chaos, not at all, things seem to be placed or stacked as best as possible, but there is very little space in-between them to move one without the other. "I am an impulsive collector," admits Jim with a smile as he prepares a cuppa for the author and himself. Jim immediately comes across as a nice approachable guy who is not at all bothered by the presence of inquisitive visitors armed with tape recorder and camera equipment. He seems well prepared for such events as his already half filled visitor's book testifies, not only because of his Minors, but also the extensive vintage tractor collection he once had.

Jim Speers was born in 1938 in Hastings and grew up on his parents' farm about 10 miles south of town. Despite being property owners his mother and father were not wealthy in those days and had only a Ford Model T and a Bedford truck, which Jim's Father used in his job as a

harvesting contractor. In later years things improved and they owned a Chrysler car and then moved on to Vauxhalls. From an early age young Jim developed an interest in motorcars and longed to have one himself as soon as possible, but that was out of question until he reached his teens. His first car to get around in was an old Austin 7 that had the tendency to break down regularly. Jim, being a handy sort of fellow did his own repairs and often biked into town and back to organize spares. A cousin of his was more fortunate in terms of car ownership, the family was wealthy, his Father

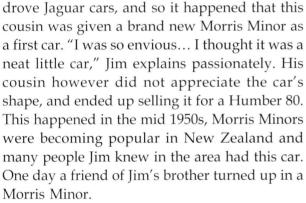

drove Jaguar cars, and so it happened that this cousin was given a brand new Morris Minor as a first car. "I was so envious… I thought it was a neat little car," Jim explains passionately. His cousin however did not appreciate the car's shape, and ended up selling it for a Humber 80. This happened in the mid 1950s, Morris Minors were becoming popular in New Zealand and many people Jim knew in the area had this car. One day a friend of Jim's brother turned up in a Morris Minor.

"This guy was very possessive and he'd never let us drive! He used to update the appearance of his model whenever cosmetic changes were introduced by the factory, so his car always looked like the latest one. This time he had fitted overriders to the bumpers and complained that he could not get the ring spanner in behind to get them uptight. Apparently it had taken him all day to fit them. When my brother and his mate were inside the house for a while, I got the socket set out, undid one overrider, turned it upside down and tightened the bolt again. When he came out I said: I like your overriders, but you've got one upside down there! That was not funny

to him and I put it right in a few minutes."

Despite growing up during the years when the Morris Minor was a common motorcar in New Zealand, Jim never drove or owned one himself. In the last decade he has made up for that. His collection started in 1990 when he purchased a Minor 1000 from a friend which came with a second body shell. Soon after that he was offered another one and could not refuse it. And so on! Undoubtedly this scenario is familiar to many readers. More followed as he became known for his hobby in the area.

"For the first few I paid quite a lot of money, often far too much, later I traded them for a dozen beers or a bottle of whiskey, but the point was to give people something for them so it was a done deal and nobody could come back years later and ask for the car back. In many cases people want to get rid of Granddad's old Morrie, because the children don't want it, it is not their type of car, and often they can't get a reply to ads in the paper either, nor do the wreckers want them these days. When they contact me I usually ask them to bring it along and a few days later there is a new arrival on the driveway. I'm just saving them from the crusher until I decide what to do with them."

In time his collection increased to 41 Morris Minors of which some are roadworthy and some are basket-cases. The collection is garnished by a dozen or so other makes and models such as an Austin 1100, a Ford Anglia, two Morris Commercials and several Honda Citys. This list is not comprehensive.

In 1996 Jim decided to build for himself a Morris Minor low-lite Tourer for club events of the Hawke's Bay Vintage Car Club of which he was a committee member at the time. The original car he selected for the conversion, a 1951 two-door saloon, was still in near rust-free condition and the decision to chop the roof off became a heart-wrenching one to make. This transition model was already equipped with the latest mudguards and grille that were available when it was assembled, but provisions were still made on the inner flitch panel to fit the earlier low-lite front. That made this part of the conversion an easy task after a good grille and guards were found. Other changes to the body shell, such as the welding-on of an original tourer windscreen frame, gussets under the dashboard and brackets on the B-posts, were done by a qualified panel beater. To Jim's amazement the strength of the body shell was such that it did not sag when the roof was cut through and possibly it requires only little reinforcement in the future. Time will tell. The biggest surprise, however, came when Jim removed the plywood headlining and several well-preserved pink coloured *Auckland Weekly* newspapers fell out, informing him about progress of the 1953 Royal Tour in New Zealand. On searching for the reasons why they were in there, Jim concluded that the roof must have been drumming and the owner, or perhaps a service agent, did the quick fix "Kiwi" style. The newspapers are now a treasured addition to his collection of other memorabilia.

When Jim purchased the Morris Minor the original type sidevalve engine was supplied in pieces and needed an overhaul. Jim's son Michael, who works as a mechanic in Hastings,

sourced the necessary parts and organized the machining to make them fit. After five days of evening work the engine was back in running condition and, according to Jim, purrs nicely. The project looks good and very tidy but now awaits trimming and finishing touches when time allows.

It was a refreshing day for the author on Jim's farm, and as we finished our talk and ventured outside for photos Jim admited: "My biggest trouble is I have too many cars and don't get to drive them very often which causes all sorts of problems; the brakes corrode and master cylinders leak, particularly in Morris Minors, so I keep saying to my wife that I won't collect any more. But if a week later something interesting comes up, and the price is right, I surely buy it!"

CHAPTER TWENTY-THREE
Nobby Stowell: Collector

When Nobby Stowell of Tauranga looks at a Morris Minor he says it reminds him of the lines of a beautiful lady. Nobby is a genuine third generation enthusiast. His grandfather, father and uncle all used to own Morris Minors. He bought his first one in 1963 and from then on he set out to collect every Morris Minor he could lay his hands on. Over the 30-odd years there were plenty available to built up a very impressive ownership record of more than 250 vehicles made between 1948 and 1974. His rural home near Tauranga was the home of about 60 permanent Morrie residents and became known to enthusiasts nation-wide as Nobby's Minor Farm. "I would do anything to get hold of Morries," he confesses with a smile, "buy, beg, or steal (not really), whatever, even one I had to drag out of a swamp! I would do anything to get them, all of them." When Nobby came home from work he often found new arrivals parked at his gate sometimes with a good bye message stuck behind the windscreen. As each new vehicle came into the yard, Nobby named it and defined its gender. That way some of them had not only been given a new name but also had a sex change, "Heck" became "Cherry" for example. One lady donor who entrusted her beloved Morrie to him could not bare the prospect of anyone taking parts off it, so Nobby obliged and simply buried the car. He is a man of practical solutions it seems and things are not taken too seriously.

Unfortunately Nobby's Minor Farm is history now, it does not exist anymore, the collection has been sold due to a change in lifestyle and partially because people begged to buy them in recent years. When asked why he has given up Morris Minors, Nobby looks askance and replies,

"I have *never* given up Morris Minors, I just got rid of some of them and I still have some here and there, and…" he adds after a pause with a big grin, "I do know where some of the others are, I might grab them back one day!"

These days Nobby says he is a handyman-cum-builder "by trade", lives in a Bedford house truck and describes himself as a Kiwi loafer who can "hit the road" any time he wants to, and be totally irresponsible (in the nicest possible way,

Part of Nobby's early collection.

The Philipino Taxi is made up from Morrie parts produced between 1948 and 1969 and includes Nissan running gear.

he means). He built himself a Morris Minor house truck first named "Strawberry Fields" and more recently renamed "Baby", because that's what "she" is compared to his bigger truck. The basis of his construction forms a 1955 Series II pick up still running on the 803cc gearbox, but its original engine has been replaced with the stronger 948cc unit to cope with the extra load. Very few modifications were needed to make this "weekender" or "shopping basket" as he calls it, legal for the road. "It is only 65kg heavier than a standard Minor Van, which turned out that way more by good luck than good management," Nobby explains in his typical "she'll be right" Kiwi style. For extra safety and comfort he has fitted 9 spring leaves and air shocks on the back

Despite its bulky appearance the suspension seems to cope very well with the load.

It took about a month to craft the steering wheel using the original steel skeleton sandwiched in wood.

suspension to prevent excessive body roll in corners and in cross winds. He is very pleased with the results and claims that it handles better than a standard van.

The accommodation part of the "camper" (sorry), clad with durable plywood, is steel framed and fastened with six bolts to the chassis frame. For safety reasons window "glass" is made from acrylic sheet and the real lead glass window is sandwiched between two sheets. Nobby took great pride in pointing out that the external colours he used and the style of the ornaments he fitted, are based on traditional ideas found in Maori culture, in particular the *whare*, the meeting house.

Some readers might get the impression that Nobby has retired from serious collecting or tinkering with Morries and spends all his time lazing around in Tauranga's sunshine, but far from it: his next project, a Morris Minor pick-up with Double-Cab is already in the planning.

Acknowledgements

Gathering the information and visuals for this book has almost been a forensic process which meant completely relying on the goodwill and resources of many people who share my interest in New Zealand's motoring history.

Without their generous help in entrusting me with their precious archives this book would have had only a few illustrations and consequently would have remained unpublished.

I want to express my sincere thanks and appreciation to the following people and organisations:

My parents, Willy and Elfriede Schoenbrunn, for their understanding and generous financial support at a difficult time of unemployment during the first four years of research for this book; my beloved wife Keiko Nojima-Schoenbrunn for her motivating when, at times, the project seemed rather overwhelming and also for her calming influence when the PC gave me a hard time; my infant son Andy with whom I did not spent as much time as I should have.

The people whose stories and photos are featured in this book:

Sir Charles J.B.Norwood, Lady R.A. Norwood, Sir Walter N. Norwood, Lady R.M. Norwood, Richard Andrews, Terry Beresford, Neville Brennan, Bruce S. Carson, Laurie Cromie, Kevin Fisher, Ross L. George, Russel Greer, Ian Hope, Eric Ludlow, John Lytollis, John B. McKillop, Jim Speers, Ron Stone, Nobby Stowell.

For their contribution in word, illustration or permission I also thank; Ken Beaver, Wilf Boyte, Jenny Brown (nee Norwood), D. Churchill, Murray Cossey, Jim Davidson, Chris Dent, Ian Drummond, Peter Etheridge, John F. Ewart, George Mck. Fraser, R. Fraser, Rex Gillcrest, Barry Gillum, Joe Harlock, Graham Hawkes, Alan Jones, Ernie Moston O.B.E., Grahame Murray, John Norwood, Stewart Park, Larry Robins O.B.E., Lester Rogers, H. Seabrook, Grant Seath, Ewan Sim, Chris Slater, Robin M. Startup, Jules Tapper, Peter Taylor, Mrs. Temperton, Norris Warren, George Weigel, John Wilson, Basil Wood.

For their technical support and cooperation I thank; Rosemary Allen (Tauranga Girl's College), Peter Balfour (Colourcraft Reproductions Ltd.), Kevin Ball (Wairarapa Times Age), Ross Bly (Wellington City Council), Alan Bryce (Invercargill Public Library), Joanne Buchanan (New Zealand Herald), Colin Campbell (Colin Campbell Motors Ltd.), A. C. Candy (Steel & Tube Holdings Ltd.), Anders Clausager (British Motor Industry Heritage Trust), Geoff Clemence (Honda Cars Ltd. Christchurch), Geoff Davies (The Dominion, Editorial Manager), Rosemary Deane (New Zealand National Maritime Museum), Ron Fox (The Evening Post, Illustrations Editor), Pam Geras (Mobil Oil New Zealand Ltd.), John Green (Mitre 10 Ltd. Invercargill), Diana Hare (Wellington Botanic Garden), Dave Harley (Honda Cars Ltd. Christchurch), Graham Harnett (Car Haulaways Ltd.), Ann Hedges (Enerco New Zealand Ltd. Auckland), Sesela Hibit (Wellington City Council, Information Management), Michelle Hill (Crippled Children Society, Information Manager), Ray Knowles (Watties New Zealand Ltd. Hastings), Charles Lacy (Car Haulaways Limited), Mary Lewis (Hocken Library, Dunedin), Clive Lind (The Evening Post, Deputy Editor), Gordon Maitland (Auckland Institute & Museum), Ronelle Maritz (Mercury Energy Ltd. Auckland), Howard Mayer (Mayer & Toye Ltd.), Joan McCracken (Alexander Turnbull Library), Peter McCurdy (New Zealand National Maritime Museum), Alan McNeill (ICI Dulux Paints Ltd.), Chris Morrisson (Union Shipping Ltd.), Greg Mulvey (Invercargill Licensing Trust), Bob Naisbitt (History House, Greymouth), Shane C. Niblock (Air Logistics N.Z. Ltd.), Joanne O'Connor (Transalta N.Z. Ltd, Wellington), Roger Page (Transalta N.Z. Ltd. Wellington), Brian Paulin (Union Shipping Ltd.), Tony Pickering (Union Shipping Ltd.), Peter Press (Norwood Farm Machinery Centre Masterton), Neil Price (Wellington City Council Photography), Karam Ram (British Motor Industry Heritage Trust), Robin Roddick (Graphics Art Technologies N.Z. Ltd.), Brian Scadden (B/W Photo Restoration and Printing), Ken Scadden (Wellington Maritime Museum Director), David Scadden (Computer Wizard), Michael Smith (The Dominion, Illustrations Editor), Barbara Spiers (Auckland Institute & Museum), Carolyn Stringer (Auckland City Libraries), Roscoe Turner (Shell Heritage Society), Kerry Waite (Norwood Farm Machinery Centre, Palmerston North), Hans Weichselbaum (Digital-Image N.Z. Ltd. Auckland),

Wellington Free Ambulance (the Board of Management and Author of *Borne Free* A.W. Beasley) Felicity Wilson (Motor Trade Association Inc.), Gareth Winter (Wairarapa Archive).

I have made every effort to trace, in order to thank and acknowledge, the photographers whose material I have reproduced; but after the lapse of many decades I have not always had success. To those individuals, their descendents, and organisations whom I have been unable to trace I here express my thanks and appreciation: F.G. Barker, R.D. Doig, Earle Andrew, Green & Hahn, Hazledine's Studio Ltd, Kenneth Alexander, Photo News Ltd, South Pacific Photos, Sparrow Pictures Ltd, Vahry-Sindall.

My heartfelt apologies go out to those people who have given their time for interviews and photo sessions, but their stories did not make it into this book, because the archival material available was greater than initially expected and that had to be given priority over more recent content. I thank: Ken Bucknell, Ted Dixon, Graham Martin, Alison Mehaffey, Dr Ross Sheppard, Robert Simondsen, and Kevin Sketchley.

"MM 50", pictured on the front cover, was mechanically restored by Jim Kerrick of Wanganui.

A special thanks to Roma and Richard Scadden for being wonderful friends and for giving me the freedom to build my car collection and, consequently, develop my interest in New Zealand motoring history.

Reiner Schoenbrunn

Index